IMAGES
of America

LIGHTHOUSES AND LIFESAVING STATIONS ON CAPE ANN

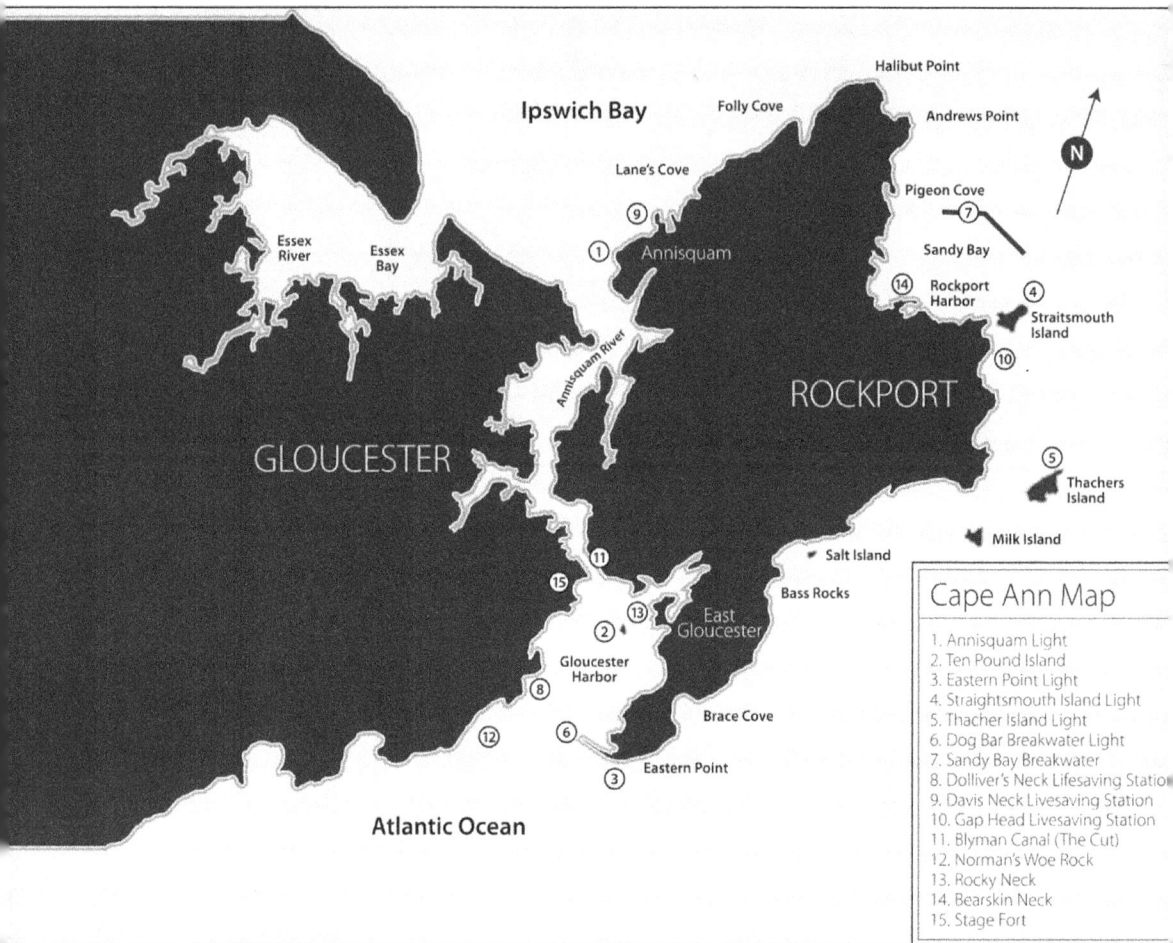

Cape Ann Map

1. Annisquam Light
2. Ten Pound Island
3. Eastern Point Light
4. Straightsmouth Island Light
5. Thacher Island Light
6. Dog Bar Breakwater Light
7. Sandy Bay Breakwater
8. Dolliver's Neck Lifesaving Station
9. Davis Neck Livesaving Station
10. Gap Head Livesaving Station
11. Blyman Canal (The Cut)
12. Norman's Woe Rock
13. Rocky Neck
14. Bearskin Neck
15. Stage Fort

This map highlights the important places noted in this book, including the lighthouses, lifesaving stations, and other landmarks associated with Cape Ann. Samuel De Champlain referred to Cape Ann as the "Cap aux Isles" or "Cape of Islands," which included Straitsmouth, Thacher, and Milk Islands. The personal narrative of his exploits was first printed in 1613. (Author's collection.)

ON THE COVER: This 1889 photograph shows two gentlemen looking across to Thacher Island. It was taken by Joseph H. Clark, a local Cape Ann photographer. The location was at Emerson Point, just south of Loblolly Cove in Rockport. (Cape Ann Museum.)

IMAGES
of America

LIGHTHOUSES AND LIFESAVING STATIONS ON CAPE ANN

Paul St. Germain

ARCADIA
PUBLISHING

Published by Arcadia Publishing
Charleston, South Carolina

Library of Congress Control Number: 2013932656

For all general information, please contact Arcadia Publishing:
Telephone 843-853-2070
Fax 843-853-0044
E-mail sales@arcadiapublishing.com
For customer service and orders:
Toll-Free 1-888-313-2665

Visit us on the Internet at www.arcadiapublishing.com

*To my wife, Betty Ann, who has been my lifesaver
and my guiding light for 50 years*

CONTENTS

Acknowledgments   6

Introduction   7

1.   Cape Ann: "Cape of Islands"   9

2.   Ten Pound Island Light Station: "Le Beauport"   17

3.   Eastern Point Light Station: "The Ruby Light"   33

4.   Annisquam Light Station: "Squam Light"   47

5.   Straitsmouth Light Station: "The Cove"   59

6.   Cape Ann Light Station: "Thacher's Woe"   73

7.   Gap Cove Lifesaving Station: "The Gap"   91

8.   Davis Neck Lifesaving Station: "Bay View"   105

9.   Dolliver's Neck Lifesaving Station: "Norman's Woe"   117

Bibliography   126

About the Thacher Island Association   127

ACKNOWLEDGMENTS

This is my second book about lighthouses. Although I learned much about developing a vintage photograph book, I am amazed at how different each one has been. Collecting the photographs has to be the most challenging part. I am deeply grateful to Fred Buck and his wife, Stephanie, at the Cape Ann Museum Library in Gloucester. While Fred searched the museum's vast collection of digital photographs, Stephanie led me in the right direction time and again to include the correct information for each photograph. I appreciate Fred's patience and intimate knowledge of this wonderful collection. I also appreciate Stephanie's intuitive knowledge of the library. She would bringing me books or documents and say, "You might find this useful," even before I had asked her about a particular subject.

Gwen Stephenson of the Sandy Bay Historical Society was most helpful in allowing me free access to its enormous collection of glass-plate negatives, photographs, and books and in allowing me to scan whatever I needed. Chris Havern, the US Coast Guard historian, did everything with me by e-mail, supplying very rich historic lighthouse information. Jeremy D'Entremont, lighthouse expert and author, was helpful in allowing me to use much of the information he has gathered over the years in producing his own series of lighthouse books.

Bob Ambrogi, who runs a blog, Vintage Rockport, was a valuable and friendly helper in supplying some of his vast collection of vintage postcards as well as the information to go along with them. Martha Oaks, the curator of the Cape Ann Museum, allowed me to use many of the Fitz Henry Lane paintings that highlight various Cape Ann locations. Jim Claflin informed me when he came across photographs or documents related to my subjects from his collection of lighthouse and lifesaving artifacts, literature, and documents. Mary Palmstrom was very generous in supplying me with many of her stereopticon slides. Sarah Dunlop, of the Gloucester Archives, directed me to vital information about life on Cape Ann in the 1800s. George Grimes, who wrote a book about his seafaring career, gave me a number of lifesaving station crew photographs he had from his grandfather, a surfman at Gap Head Cove here in Rockport.

And, of course, I wish most of all to thank my wife, Betty Ann, for putting up with my being sequestered at my computer for hours and days at a time and then having the patience to read, edit, and critique my work. Thank you all!

Most of the images in this volume appear courtesy of the Cape Ann Museum (CAM), the Sandy Bay Historical Society (SBHS), the US Coast Guard Historian's Office (USCG), and the Thacher Island Association (TIA).

INTRODUCTION

Cape Ann, located about 35 miles north of Boston, includes the coastal towns of Rockport, Gloucester, Magnolia, Manchester-by-the-Sea, and parts of Essex. It is well known for its fishing industry, granite quarries, shipbuilding, unique topography, unusual landmarks, and artist colonies and famous plein air atmosphere. This book focuses on the "island" of Cape Ann, which encompasses most of Gloucester and Rockport. This area, of about 25 square miles, is separated from the mainland by the Annisquam River, which is a tidal, saltwater estuary. This barrier makes most of Cape Ann an island. As one circumnavigates the 18 miles of the cape's shoreline, one notices the many rocks, reefs, beaches, ledges, shoals, and hidden dangers of sunken wrecks. It is one of the most dangerous maritime areas on coastal Massachusetts. Cape Ann extends about 10 miles farther out into the Atlantic Ocean than does the rest of Massachusetts, with the exception of the other cape, Cape Cod.

Surrounded on three sides by the ocean, is it any wonder that this small area has six lighthouses, three lifesaving stations (at one time, there were six), a US Coast Guard station, hundreds of buoys, breakwaters, and channel markers? All of these features have been designed for the safety of mariners and fishermen, who have navigated these waters in increasing numbers since the 1600s. The first lighthouses built on Thacher Island, in 1771, were erected at the request of colonial shipping interests who petitioned the Massachusetts government. John Hancock had a large shipping business in the area and was influential in convincing the British-controlled Massachusetts Bay Colony to build two lights on Thacher Island.

The same year that my book *Twin Lights of Thacher Island, Cape Ann* was published, an announcement was made by the US Coast Guard and the National Park Service that the lighthouse on Straitsmouth Island was to be offered for ownership to any individual or group that would agree to its maintenance and restoration. This was in accordance with the National Historic Lighthouse Preservation Act, passed by Congress in 2000, which gave the Coast Guard and General Services Administration authority to dispose of active lighthouses to the private sector upon agreement by the recipients to maintain them.

The Thacher Island Association, a nonprofit fundraising group dedicated to restoring and maintaining the Cape Ann Light Station on Thacher Island, thought this was a great opportunity for the Town of Rockport to own the Straitsmouth lighthouse. Located about a mile from Rockport Harbor, it provides an iconic and scenic view from the town, just as Thacher Island does.

The town's board of selectmen agreed, the application was submitted, and, in September 2010, Secretary of the Interior Ken Salazar confirmed the transfer of the lighthouse to the town, which accepted the tower and the 1.8 acres of land it stood on in July 2011.

While researching the history of Straitsmouth, I began to look into the three other lighthouses, along with their relationship to the three lifesaving stations on Cape Ann. My research led me to discover some very interesting facts and vintage photographs of Ten Pound Island, Annisquam, and Eastern Point Light Stations, as well as Davis Neck, Dolliver's Neck, and Gap Head Lifesaving Stations. This book is the culmination of those efforts. I hope you enjoy it.

One

Cape Ann
"Cape of Islands"

This Cape Ann Chamber of Commerce advertisement from 1927 shows that the Cape Ann area was an attractive tourist destination and relied on its fishing, shipbuilding, granite cutting, and artistic heritage to draw people from around the country. Tourism became a major industry when the Eastern Railroad extended its lines from Boston into Gloucester and Rockport in the 1840s. (CAM.)

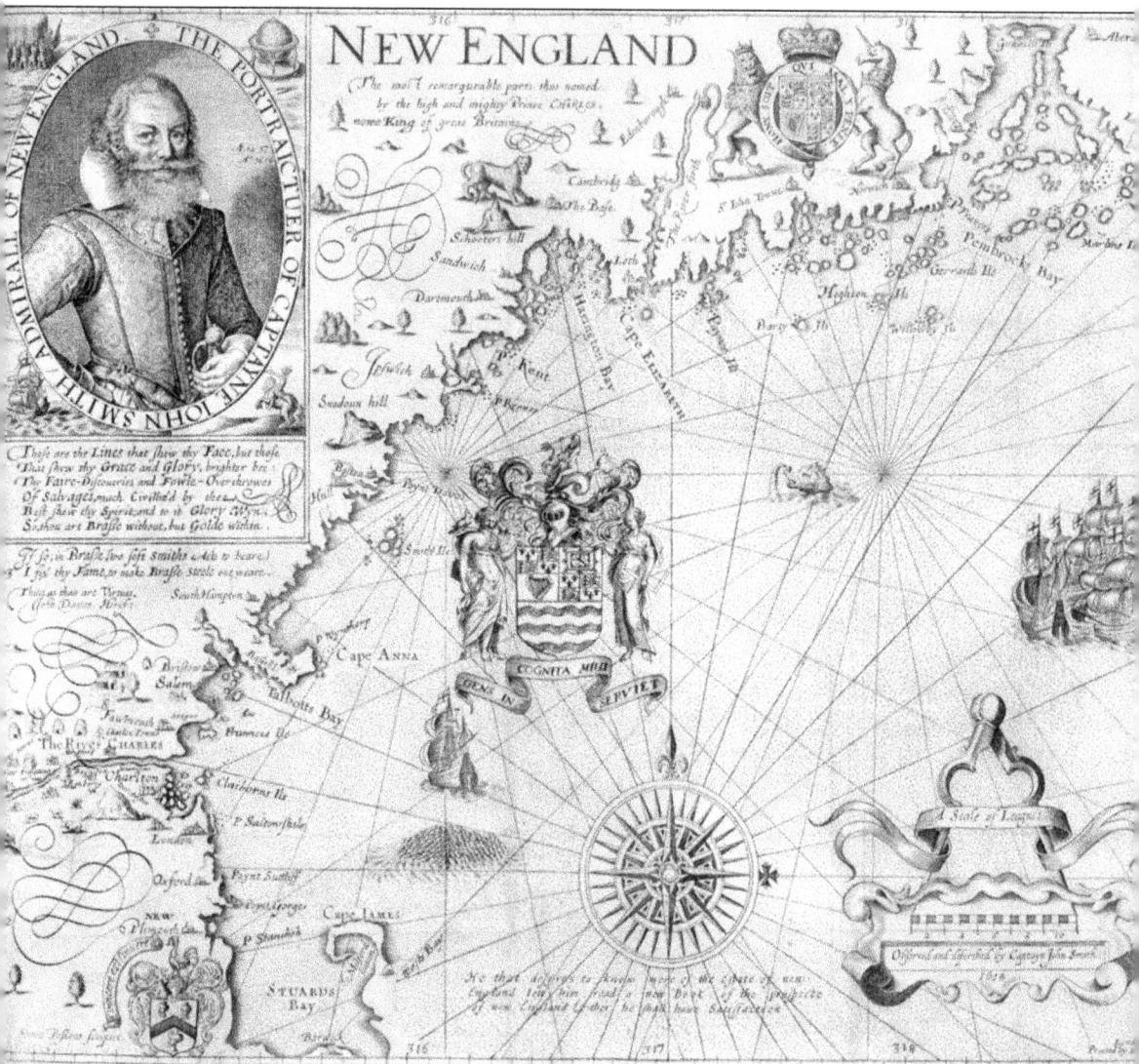

John Smith (1580–1631) was a soldier, explorer, author, and leader of the Virginia Colony (Jamestown) in 1607. He was hired by King James I of England to explore the coast of Maine and Massachusetts in 1614. He named the area New England. Upon his arrival, he discovered Cape Ann, which he then named Cape Tragabigzanda after a kindly princess who cared for him while he was a prisoner of the Turks years earlier. When Smith presented this chart to James I, the king changed its name to Cape Ann in honor of his wife, Anne of Denmark. Smith participated in jousts with Turkish soldiers and succeeded in decapitating three of them. Prince Bathory, his patron, rewarded him with a patent for a coat of arms bearing three Turks' heads on a shield. While exploring Massachusetts Bay in 1614, Smith came across three islands, which he named the Turks Heads. The islands' profiles reminded him of the turbans worn by the Turks. Those islands are today named Straitsmouth, Milk, and Thacher. (CAM.)

Gloucester is America's oldest seaport, dating to 1623. The first settlers were members of the Dorchester Company from England, primarily fishermen and farmers. The first fish stage was set up at Stage Fort Park in Gloucester, signaling the start of the fishing industry that has gone uninterrupted since. In 1859, the heyday of Gloucester fishing, there were 301 schooners crewed by 3,588 men and boys. (Library of Congress.)

The Gloucester Fisherman's Memorial cenotaph sculpture was created by the English sculptor Leonard Craske (1882–1950) and installed in 1925. This eight-foot-tall bronze statue honors the fishermen of Cape Ann. It was modeled after Capt. Clayton Morrissey, a famous Gloucester fisherman who captained the schooner *Effie M. Morrissey*. It depicts a fisherman dressed in oilskins at the wheel of his vessel looking across Gloucester Harbor. (CAM.)

The first fishing schooner was built in 1713 by Capt. Andrew Robinson. As she left the launching ways, a spectator cried, "See how she scoons!" Robinson shouted in reply, "A schooner let her be!" By 1741, about 70 of these craft were fishing each summer on the far-off Grand Bank of Newfoundland. Then, and for many years to come, the crews fished with hook and line. (CAM.)

The clipper *Grace L. Fears*, shown here being built at the David Story Yard in Vincent's Cove, was launched on July 2, 1874. Shipbuilding, a vast enterprise on Cape Ann, occurred in Essex, Gloucester, Annisquam, and Rockport. Chebacco boats, schooners, sloops, square riggers, and pinkies were built by families named Burnham, Story, James, Bishop, Woodbury, Irving, McManus, and Adams, to name a few. There were 10 shipyards in Essex alone. Howard Blackburn and Tom Welch went astray from this clipper while fishing off Newfoundland in a January 1883 blizzard. (CAM.)

The schooner *Arethusa* was launched on September 25, 1907. Designed by famous architect Thomas F. McManus and built in the Tarr & James Yard in Essex, she was 114 feet long. The original owner was Capt. Clayton Morrissey, who eventually sold her to the rumrunner Capt. "Wild Bill" McCoy, who changed her name to *Tomaka*. She was lost in Halifax on November 8, 1929. (CAM.)

The schooner *Adventure* was designed by Thomas McManus as a "knockabout"—without a bowsprit for the safety of the crew. Built in 1926 in Essex by the John F. James & Son Shipyard, she measured 121.6 feet in length and had a gross tonnage of 130. Carrying a sailing rig, diesel engine, and 14 dories, *Adventure* was an exceptionally fast and able vessel, the ultimate evolution of the fishing schooner. She was a "highliner," the biggest moneymaker of all time, landing nearly $4 million worth of cod and halibut during her fishing career. When retired in 1953, *Adventure* was the last American dory fishing trawler left in the Atlantic. She has been designated a National Historic Landmark and is on display at the Gloucester Maritime Museum in the harbor. (CAM.)

Cape Ann granite is well known around the nation. The industry started inconspicuously in 1800, but at its height, over 50 quarries existed, employing over 1,000 men. Paving blocks were the mainstay of the trade. Cape Ann granite paved the streets of Boston, New York, Philadelphia, New Orleans, and San Francisco. The first paving blocks came from Flat Ledge Quarry and were shipped aboard the sloop *Fox* to be used at Fort Warren on George's Island in Boston Harbor. (SBHS.)

The fishing shack on the left, known as Motif No. 1, is reputed to be the most painted building in America. Built in the 1840,s as Rockport became home to a colony of fishermen and artists, it is still a favorite subject of painters and photographers. Although destroyed in a 1978 blizzard, it was rebuilt using the original plans and was once featured on a US postage stamp. (SBHS.)

Artists' Row   Bearskin Neck, Rockport, Mass.

Artists' studios are now housed in many of the original fishermen shacks that occupied this area starting in the early 1800s. It is said that 5,000 artists visit Cape Ann each year and that fully 500 make their homes here. This c. 1901 postcard view shows some of the studios on Bearskin Neck in Rockport. (SBHS.)

THE ARTISTS' CORNER   BEARSKIN NECK   ROCKPORT, MASS.

This postcard shows an artist in the foreground painting the famous Motif No. 1 in an area once called the "Artist's Corner." It is believed that the artist Lester Hornby (1882–1956) dubbed the old fish shack "Motif No. 1" while conducting art classes for his young students. (SBHS.)

Fitz Henry Lane (1804–1865) immortalized the town of Gloucester in numerous paintings from 1848 until his death. Schooners, fishing vessels, harbors, and coves all appeared in his work. Lane was a leader in the art tradition called luminism and put Cape Ann on the art-historical map. Other famous artists who lived on Cape Ann at various times were Winslow Homer, Edward Hopper, and Marsden Hartley. (CAM.)

The "summer people" began to arrive in large numbers on Cape Ann when the Eastern Railroad completed its link to Gloucester via its inland track in 1847. The cape's many beaches were a major attraction. The dramatic increase in the construction of summer cottages and hotel accommodations in the third quarter of the 19th century has made Cape Ann a premier vacation destination up to the present day. (SBHS.)

16

Two

TEN POUND ISLAND
LIGHT STATION
"LE BEAUPORT"

The Ten Pound Island Light Station was established in 1821 to safely guide mariners into Gloucester's inner harbor. It has witnessed stately schooners and historic vessels make their way to sea every day for over a century. The first lighthouse, lit in October 1821, was a 20-foot-tall, conical stone tower. (CAM.)

Ten Pound is a three-and-a-half-acre island located at the eastern end of Gloucester Harbor, with shoals between it and the mainland to the east. There are two stories about how it received its name. One account has it that £10 was the amount of money the early settlers paid the local American Indian tribe for the island. Another claims that the name refers to the number of sheep pens the island could hold. In Colonial times, the community formally reserved the island for a ram pasture containing 10 "pounds," or pens. A person landing on the island in 1644 would have seen a sign that read, "Ten Pound Island is reserved for rams onlie; and whoever shall put anie but Great Ramms shall forfeit 2s, 6d per head." In the photograph, note that the lantern room was changed from the original "birdcage" design. (USCG.)

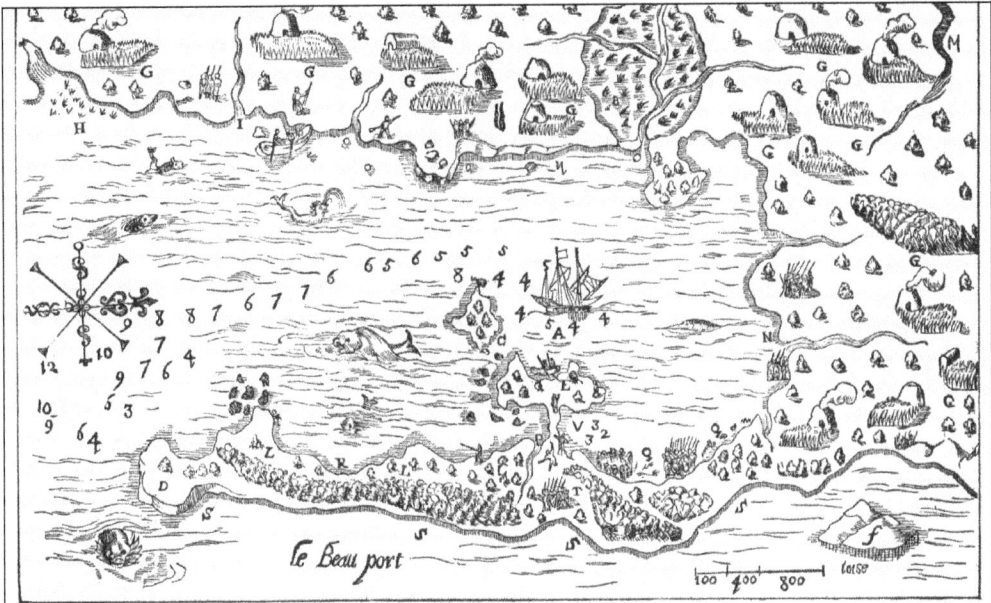

Champlain drew this map of Gloucester Harbor, which he called "Le Beauport," in 1606. His ship was anchored at "A," and "C" marks Little Island (Ten Pound Island). (CAM.)

Amos Story served as keeper of Ten Pound Island Lighthouse from 1833 to 1849 and was one of the many witnesses who reported a sea serpent near the island in 1817. On August 10, Story reported a "strange marine animal. . . . His head appeared shaped much like that of a sea turtle, and he carried his head from ten to twelve inches above the surface of the water." This lithograph is dated August 23, 1817. (CAM.)

19

The present conical cast-iron tower replaced the original stone tower in 1881. Resting on a brick foundation, the tower is 30 feet tall and topped with a fifth-order Fresnel lens. It stands 43 feet above the sea at mean high water. The tower is painted an unusual brown color. Other associated buildings include a granite oil house from 1821 (not shown) and a two-story keeper's dwelling. (USCG.)

Gloucester Harbor consists of two harbors. The outer harbor is a large anchoring basin formerly called the "Southwest Harbor" that, since 1904, has been protected by the Dog Bar Breakwater at Eastern Point (seen here in the far distance). The inner harbor was afforded additional protection from heavy seas by Ten Pound Island and Rocky Neck. (CAM.)

Shag rock can be seen in the right foreground. The lighthouse contained a fifth-order Fresnel lens that revolved with a white flash every five seconds. It has been removed and is thought to be at the Maine Lighthouse Museum in Rockland, Maine, although it is not identified as such among the museum's many fifth-order lenses. (CAM.)

This 1890 photograph of a schooner sailing by Ten Pound Island and the fish hatchery was taken from the area called the Fort, originally called Watch House Point. In 1743, a breastwork was erected and eight 12-pound cannon were installed on the point to protect ships in the inner harbor from enemy warships and pirates. (CAM.)

This panoramic photograph of Ten Pound Island includes the fish hatchery (left), the radio compass station antenna (center), and the cluster of keeper's house, lighthouse, and pyramid-shaped bell tower. A US Fish Commission Hatchery was constructed on the island in 1889 and abandoned and closed in 1940. Fish eggs were collected aboard fishing schooners by hatchery staff, transported to Ten Pound Island, and, after hatching, released three to five miles east of

Gloucester Harbor. It was estimated that one cod lays three to nine million eggs a year, taking two to three weeks to hatch. This hatchery specialized in cod, pollock, halibut, and lobsters in its 50 years of existence. (Author's collection.)

The purse seiner *William M. Gaffney* passes by Ten Pound Island in 1890. She was built in Vincent Cove by David A. Story in 1877 and sailed until 1900. She was an extreme clipper that fished for mackerel under Capt. John W. McFarlane. In the US Fish Commission bulletin of 1889, it was reported that she arrived in port with 450 barrels of mackerel. Today, a model of the *Gaffney* is in the Sawyer Free Library in Gloucester. (CAM.)

This aerial photograph of Ten Pound Island was taken in the winter of 1930. The fish hatchery is visible at the top of the island. The US Commission of Fish and Fisheries (later the US Bureau of Fisheries) was established in 1871. It reported in 1884 that 473 vessels employed 6,436 men out of Gloucester that year. In 1883, 61 million cod, 50 million haddock, and 9 million halibut were caught. (USCG.)

The island reached its heyday in the early 1930s, when a dozen or more buildings dotted its three and a half acres. This 1950 photograph was taken just seven years before the island was abandoned. Most of its buildings have been razed or allowed to crumble. In 1977, a city crew removed much of the debris. The island is gradually returning to its natural state, with only the light tower and oil house remaining. (CAM.)

American artist Winslow Homer (1836–1910) lived in Gloucester on two different occasions: the summer of 1873 and again in 1880, when he stayed with the lighthouse keeper on the island. The keeper's wife was related to a friend of Homer's and took boarders in a small cottage on the island. Homer did his first watercolor series here and produced over 100 paintings and drawings of Gloucester Harbor during his stay. (Bowdoin College Museum of Art.)

The history of Gloucester fisheries has been written in tears. In 1873, thirty-one vessels never returned. On August 24, 1873, in a single storm, 128 men were lost. Homer perfected his skills as a preeminent marine painter at Gloucester. In this 1873 oil painting, entitled *Dad's Coming!*, Homer shows the hopes and fears of a family awaiting the return of a loved one. (CAM.)

Homer began his career as an illustrator for *Harper's Weekly*. This wood engraving for the October 11, 1873, edition is titled *Shipbuilding, Gloucester Harbor*. This shipyard was like a fairyland to the town's children. They gathered after school to question workmen and to build their own miniature vessels. The *Harper's* story went on to explain that the American shipyards, especially in Gloucester, were expanding to resume their former supremacy. (Author's collection.)

26

Fitz Henry Lane was charmed by Ten Pound Island, featuring it in at least five of his oil paintings. This one, entitled *Ten Pound Island from Pavilion Beach*, is on display at the Cape Ann Museum. Lane was born in Gloucester on December 19, 1804. Paralyzed at the age of 18 months, he never regained the use of his legs. Denied the usual activities of childhood, Lane turned to drawing. He lived in a granite house he built on Duncan's Point, where he had a commanding view of Gloucester Harbor. (CAM.)

The US Coast Guard established the first air station on Ten Pound Island in 1925 with one small scout plane. The initial purpose of the operation was to catch rumrunners in the area during Prohibition. In 1925, Lt. Comdr. Carl C. von Paulsen, on his own initiative, acquired a 200-horsepower Navy Vought UO-1 seaplane that had been declared surplus. (CAM.)

A large surplus tent was acquired from the Army for $1, and this became the hangar. Von Paulsen began flight operations out of the Naval Reserve Air Station at Squantam, Massachusetts, before moving to Ten Pound Island in 1925. (CAM.)

Von Paulsen and Ens. Leonard M. Melka flew together, searching at sea for rumrunners and keeping tabs on patrol boats. As a result of von Paulsen's successful efforts demonstrating the usefulness of aerial flight for Coast Guard operations, the service purchased five Loening OL-5 amphibians, three of which were sent to Ten Pound Island and two to Cape May, New Jersey. (CAM.)

In this aerial photograph of Ten Pound Island, the hangar tent and utility sheds are visible on the upper right, the fish hatchery is on the upper left, and the lighthouse is at lower left. Note, at left, the wing of the biplane from which this photograph was taken around 1925. (CAM.)

Rumrunner William "Wild Bill" McCoy, operating out of Gloucester, bought the schooner *Arethusa* and placed it under British registry in order to avoid being subjected to US law. He smuggled liquor from Nassau and the Bahamas, anchored in international waters, and sold the products to smaller ships that transferred it to shore. He was captured by the US Coast Guard cutter *Seneca* on November 23, 1923. (CAM.)

Gloucester Harbor has been affected by ice throughout the years. In this c. 1918 photograph taken from Fort Wharf, a steamer is hauling a schooner through ice by Ten Pound Island. (CAM.)

The schooner *Marjie Turner* (at right) of Portland, Maine, is seen at Montgomery Coal Wharf on January 21, 1912. The ship is iced in at Smith Cove as three boys skate on the frozen harbor. In January 1875, the harbor was frozen to a depth of 16 inches. In 1917, it was frozen all the way to the Eastern Point Breakwater, and the "Cut" (Blynman Canal) was shut down for six weeks. (CAM.)

These four women were office workers from George Perkins & Son, Rowe Square. They were taking a stroll on the frozen harbor near the fish hatchery and Ten Pound Island Light on February 17, 1918. (CAM.)

The schooner *America*, captained by Gil Lafford, ran aground on Ten Pound Island on September 6, 1941. (CAM.)

Ten Pound Island Light Station was decommissioned in 1956 and replaced by a modern optic atop an old bell tower. The same optic was subsequently moved to a skeleton tower on the island. The original Fresnel lens was removed from the lantern and is currently on display at the Maine Lighthouse Museum in Rockland, Maine. The keeper's dwelling was razed in 1965. (USCG.)

Ten Pound Island Lighthouse was renovated and relit as an active aid to navigation on August 7, 1989. Sen. Edward M. Kennedy spoke at the re-commissioning ceremony, remarking, "It has watched over the Gloucester fishermen who braved the wind and waves to make their living. For some of those brave souls this . . . vista of Ten Pound Island was their final vision of land." Today, only the lighthouse and the c. 1905 oil house remain. (Author's collection.)

Three

Eastern Point Light Station
"The Ruby Light"

Eastern Point Light Station, at the entrance to Gloucester Harbor, was established and lighted on January 1, 1832. A stone lighthouse 30 feet high was erected at a cost of $2,450 to help fishermen and others enter Gloucester Harbor. The first keeper was Samuel Wonson, who was hired at an annual salary of $400. (Jeremy D'Entremont.)

Tower Rebuilt 1890

The area had been home to farms, a quarry, a Civil War fort, and the Eastern Point Yacht Club. It appears that oak trees served as the first landmarks. In 1829, the Boston Marine Society said that the "erection of a monument on Eastern Point, Cape Ann, would be highly useful to navigation in Boston Bay—the old landmarks of Trees being nearly decayed and gone." (USCG.)

Following the arrival of the railroad in Gloucester in 1847, the fishing business exploded, and the importance of Eastern Point Light increased. A new 34-foot light tower replaced the poorly constructed original tower in 1848. This second Eastern Point Light became known as the "ruby light." It exhibited a fixed red light, produced in France using red plate glass surrounding 11 whale oil lamps and reflectors. (Mary Palmstrom.)

In 1857, a fourth-order Fresnel lens was installed, increasing visibility from 11 miles to 13 miles. Barbier, Renard, & Turenne of Paris, France, built this square boxed lens, which was mounted on a revolving mechanism. The lens is currently exhibited at the Cape Ann Historical Museum in Gloucester. In 1882, the characteristic of the light was changed from fixed to flashing red. (Author's collection.)

The revolving light was turned by a clockwork mechanism that had to be periodically wound by the keeper. This is a photograph from the official price list of standard articles of the Lighthouse Service general depot of 1901, showing a lens, pedestal, and ball bearing winding mechanism similar to the one used at Eastern Point Light. (James Claflin.)

The third and current lighthouse was built in 1890 on the foundation of the 1832 tower. The 36-foot brick lighthouse was attached to the keeper's house by a covered walkway. Telephone lines were added in 1896, and electricity was introduced the following year. A hand-operated fog bell was installed in 1857 in this tower. When city waterlines came to Eastern Point in 1907, a 4,000-pound, steam-driven fog bell was put into operation. (USCG.)

Located on the rocks just below Eastern Point Light, left of the flagpole in this photograph, can be seen the profile image of a woman's face. This geologic feature, named "Mother Ann" by the locals, has been featured in postcards and tourism brochures. (CAM.)

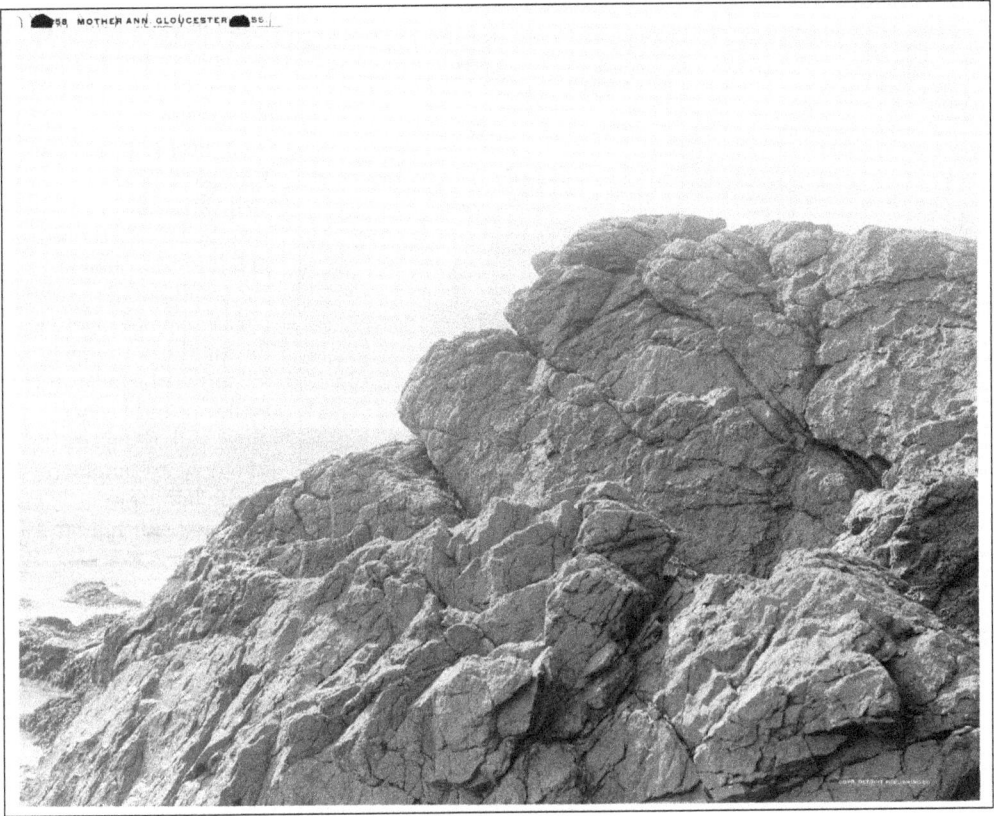

Mother Ann's profile can be clearly seen in this photograph. Just offshore is a whistling buoy, sometimes called "Mother Ann's Cow." (CAM.)

A breakwater was built between 1894 and 1905 that extended from the lighthouse to mark the Dog Bar reef. The Rockport granite structure is 2,250 feet long and 7 feet wide and cost $300,000 to erect. The breakwater's substructure is a rubble mound covered with 231,756 tons of Cape Ann granite blocks, each weighing 12 to 13 tons. Before the breakwater was completed, 40 vessels had foundered there. (CAM.)

A light was established at the end of the barrier, called the Gloucester Breakwater Light. This 1914 photograph was taken before radio antennas were installed. Note the fog bell hanging outside the small building. The bar becomes dangerous during the winter, when ice forms on the granite walkway and keepers must walk the gauntlet to tend the equipment in the light tower. (Jeremy D'Entremont.)

The two-story duplex keeper's house that stands today was built in 1879. The oil house survives from 1894, but the garage and fog signal building are more recent, erected in 1947 and 1951, respectively. In this photograph of Eastern Point Light, a horse and buggy can be seen on the far right. (Library of Congress.)

Dog Bar Breakwater constituted an uncharted reef. Capt. H.M. Godfrey of the schooner *Eleanora Van Dusen* discovered this when he tried to make safe harbor the evening of September 19, 1900. Sailing from Bay View loaded with 23,000 paving blocks and 82 tons of rough granite, he ducked into the harbor because of the weather, and he met disaster. The *Van Dusen* was the 27th craft to strike the submerged breakwater since construction on it had begun. (CAM.)

The schooner *Clara Jane* is shown here wrecked at Eastern Point on January 10, 1913. In 1906, a tripod with a fixed white light was installed and became known as the Gloucester Breakwater Light, or Dog Bar Light. After the Dog Bar Light was built, the station was required to add an assistant keeper to keep the light cleaned and filled with oil. (CAM.)

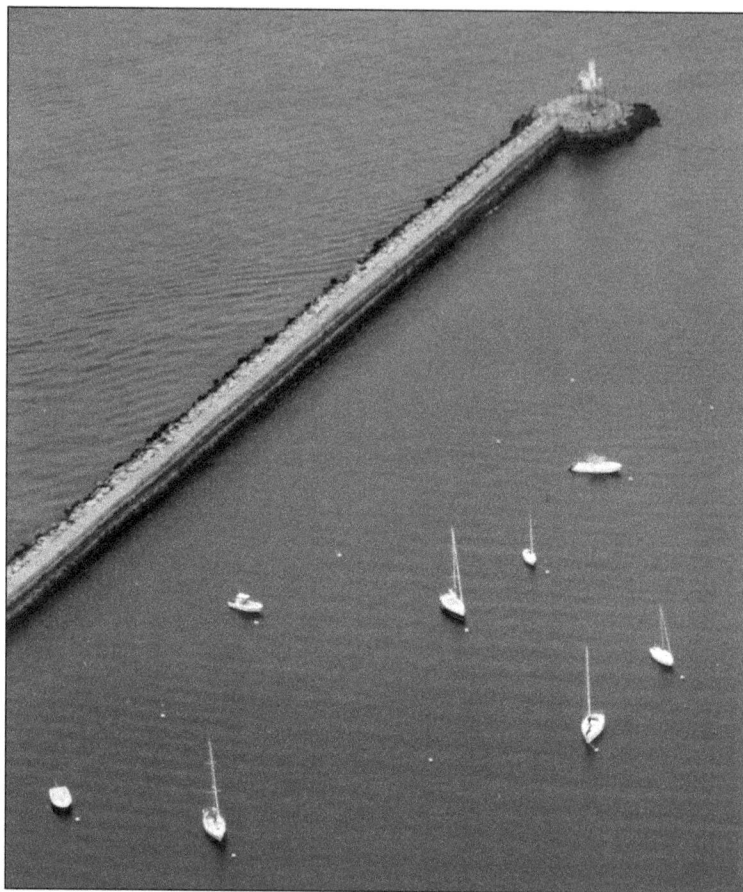

Eastern Point Light was automated in September 1985. Carroll Wonson, the great-great-great-grandson of the first keeper, Samuel Wonson, was given the honor of being the last person to manually turn on the light. (Jeremy D'Entremont.)

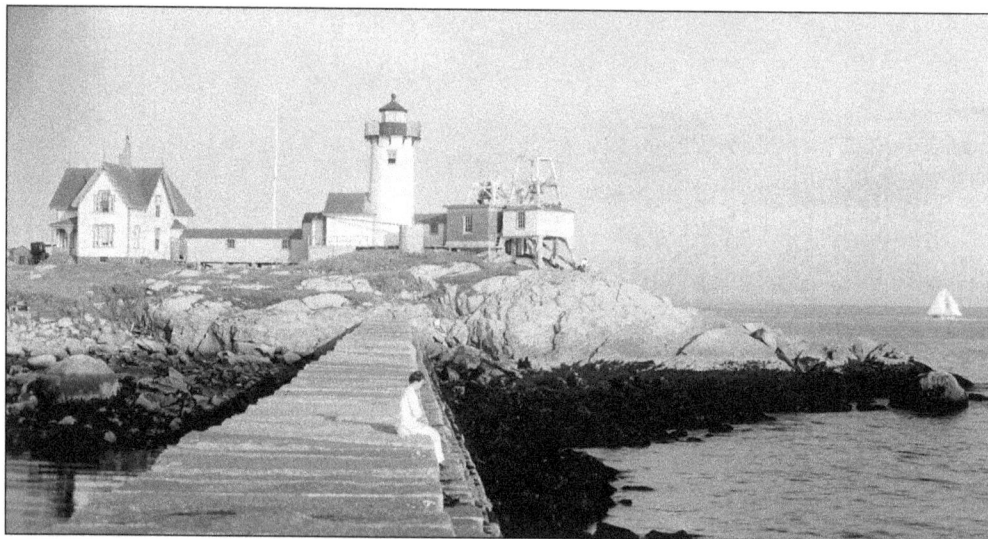

Note that there are two fog signal bells and towers on the lighthouse. One of these bells was used as the fog signal on Eastern Point Lighthouse from June 1930 to December 1969. It was cast in Chelsea, Massachusetts. Gold dust was sprinkled in the mold in order to obtain the right tone. This 4,000-pound bell struck double blows every 20 seconds. (CAM.)

Herman Spooner took this photograph of his wife, Sarah (standing), and sister on the breakwater in 1907. Shipwrecks were common before the breakwater was completed in 1905. The schooner *Carrie L. Hix* struck on January 1, 1900. On December 5, 1902, the schooner *Fio F. Macher* suffered the same fate. The *Macher* was a total loss, but all aboard were rescued by the crew of Dolliver's Neck Lifesaving Station and housed by keeper George F. Bailey at Eastern Point Light. (CAM.)

This Ernest L. Blatchford photograph from 1905 shows Eastern Point from outside Dog Bar Breakwater. Note the screen, which was constructed to baffle the sound toward the sea and away from local residents' homes. (CAM.)

Steamboats began operating Gloucester-to-Boston runs as early as 1840. Here, the SS *Cape Ann* passes by Eastern Point Light, with the *Little Giant* ferry ahead of her. *Cape Ann* operated in Gloucester for 22 years, until 1917. She was then sold and renamed *Seminole* and converted to an oceangoing towboat. (CAM.)

The steamer SS *Cape Ann* was seen on a regular basis passing Eastern Point Light. Operated by the Boston & Gloucester Steamship Company, she made regular runs to Boston for a fare 50¢ each way, as noted in this advertisement from the 1905 Gloucester Board of Trade Summer Hotel Guide. (CAM.)

The SS *Cape Ann* was built in 1884 by Neafie & Levy Ship and Engine Building Company of Philadelphia. She was made of steel and was 185 feet long. Registered to hold 1,000 people, she often exceeded that number. Powered by a 1,500-horsepower vertical compound-condensing engine, the *Cape Ann* could cruise at 16 knots. Her registry with Lloyds was ended in 1926. (CAM.)

THE SCHOONER EDWARD A. HORTON.

This lithograph of the schooner *Edward A. Horton* currently resides at the Cape Ann Museum. It shows the *Horton* rounding Eastern Point Light on October 18, 1871, after her recapture from the Canadian government by Capt. Harvey Knowlton and his gallant crew of six. Knowlton and his men went to Guysboro, Nova Scotia, to steal her back on the night of October 8. The *Horton* had been seized on September 7, 1871, by the Canadian government after she was caught fishing inside the three-mile limit line along the coast of Nova Scotia. Upon her return to Gloucester, church bells pealed, cannons boomed, and people danced in the streets. Poems and songs were written about this audacious act. (CAM.)

Lucy E. Friend, home ported in Gloucester, is seen here outbound from Montgomery Coal Wharf in the early 1900s. She was 147 feet long and was one of the fastest three-masters on the Atlantic, once sailing from Pigeon Cove to Philadelphia, carrying 50,000 paving stones, in 48 hours. She was lost on November 14, 1910, and abandoned off the Virginia coast. (CAM.)

USS *Gloucester* was a 241-foot-long gunboat that had formerly been J.P. Morgan's yacht *Corsair*. Built in 1891, she was acquired by the Navy on April 23, 1898, and served in Cuban waters with the North Atlantic Fleet. She visited her namesake, Gloucester Harbor, on July 4, 1898. She was captained by Comdr. Richard Wainwright, who eventually became superintendent of the US Naval Academy. The boat was wrecked in a hurricane in Pensacola, Florida, in 1919. (CAM.)

This photograph, taken some time after 1900, shows the lighthouse and the covered walkway from the house to the tower. (SBHS.)

This 1895 view, similar to that in the previous image, was taken before the covered walkway from the lighthouse was built. (USCG.)

This 1945 Coast Guard aerial photograph shows, from left to right, Dog Bar Breakwater, the bell tower, the light tower, the enclosed walkway from the keeper's house to the tower, the radio antenna, a small oil house (at lower center), and the expanded keeper's house and utility shed (far right). (USCG.)

Eastern Point Light Station is seen here in 1980. The bell has been removed from the bell tower, and other structures have disappeared. Eastern Point Light remains an active aid to navigation, displaying a white flash every five seconds. Although the light is automated, the station is still used as billeting for a Coast Guard family. (Author's collection.)

Four

ANNISQUAM
LIGHT STATION
"SQUAM LIGHT"

VIEW OF SQUAM LIGHT.

The village of Annisquam, established in 1631, was a fishing and shipbuilding center that rivaled Gloucester in its early days. Originally called "Squam Light," the lighthouse was built on Wigwam Point, so-called because Indians met there during the summer months to catch fish and hunt. Annisquam Harbor Light Station was first established in 1801 and is one of the oldest light stations in Massachusetts. (CAM.)

On October 26, 1800, Gustavus Griffin of Gloucester deeded to the United States "six and one half acres of land at Wigwam Point, so called, in Gloucester." The consideration was "one hundred and forty dollars paid me by the United States of America." The original lighthouse had a "birdcage" lantern room. This was later replaced with a more conventional octagonal lantern, as shown here. (CAM.)

LAND CEDED TO U. STATES. *June* 12, An. 1800. 935

An ACT to cede to the United States the Jurisdiction of the Tract of Land which shall be required for the Light-House, authorized by Congress to be erected on *Wigwam-Point.*

SECT. 1. *B*E it enacted by the Senate and House of Representatives, in General Court assembled, and by the authority of the same, That the United States of *America* may purchase or take, as herein after is provided, any Tract of Land which shall be found necessary and convenient for the Light-House, authorized by Congress to be erected upon *Wigwam-Point,* in the town of *Gloucester,* within this Commonwealth ; and during the continuance of the use and appropriation aforesaid, the jurisdiction of such Tract of Land, not exceeding the quantity of seven acres for such Light-House, shall be and hereby is ceded to, and shall be in the said United States ; *Saving and provided always,* That all civil and criminal processes, issued under the authority, or by any officers of this Commonwealth, shall have full force and effect within the said Tract of Land, and any buildings which shall be there erected, this cession of jurisdiction notwithstanding.

The U. States allowed to purchase and have jurisdiction of Land on *Wigwam-Point.*

Proviso.

This document is the Commonwealth of Massachusetts act that ceded to the United States the jurisdiction of the land for the lighthouse to be erected upon Wigwam Point (or Annisquam, as it is now known). The act further cedes "the jurisdiction of such Tract of Land, not exceeding the quantity of seven acres for such Light-House." This act was passed on June 12, 1800. (Author's collection.)

Annisquam Harbor Lt. Sta. 1857-1897

The original 32-foot wooden octagonal tower was replaced in 1897 by the existing brick tower. This 1857 photograph shows the "birdcage" lantern room. The tower shined a fixed white light 40 feet above the water. A two-room wooden keeper's house was next to the tower. The first keeper was George Day, who worked for a salary of $200 per year. (CAM.)

The name *Annisquam* appears to be a combination of the word *Squam*—the local Indian word for harbor—and *Ann*, for Cape Ann. Other historians say it is an Algonquin word meaning "top of the rock." The Annisquam River is a saltwater estuary that connects Ipswich Bay to Gloucester Harbor, essentially separating most of Cape Ann from the mainland and creating an island. (CAM.)

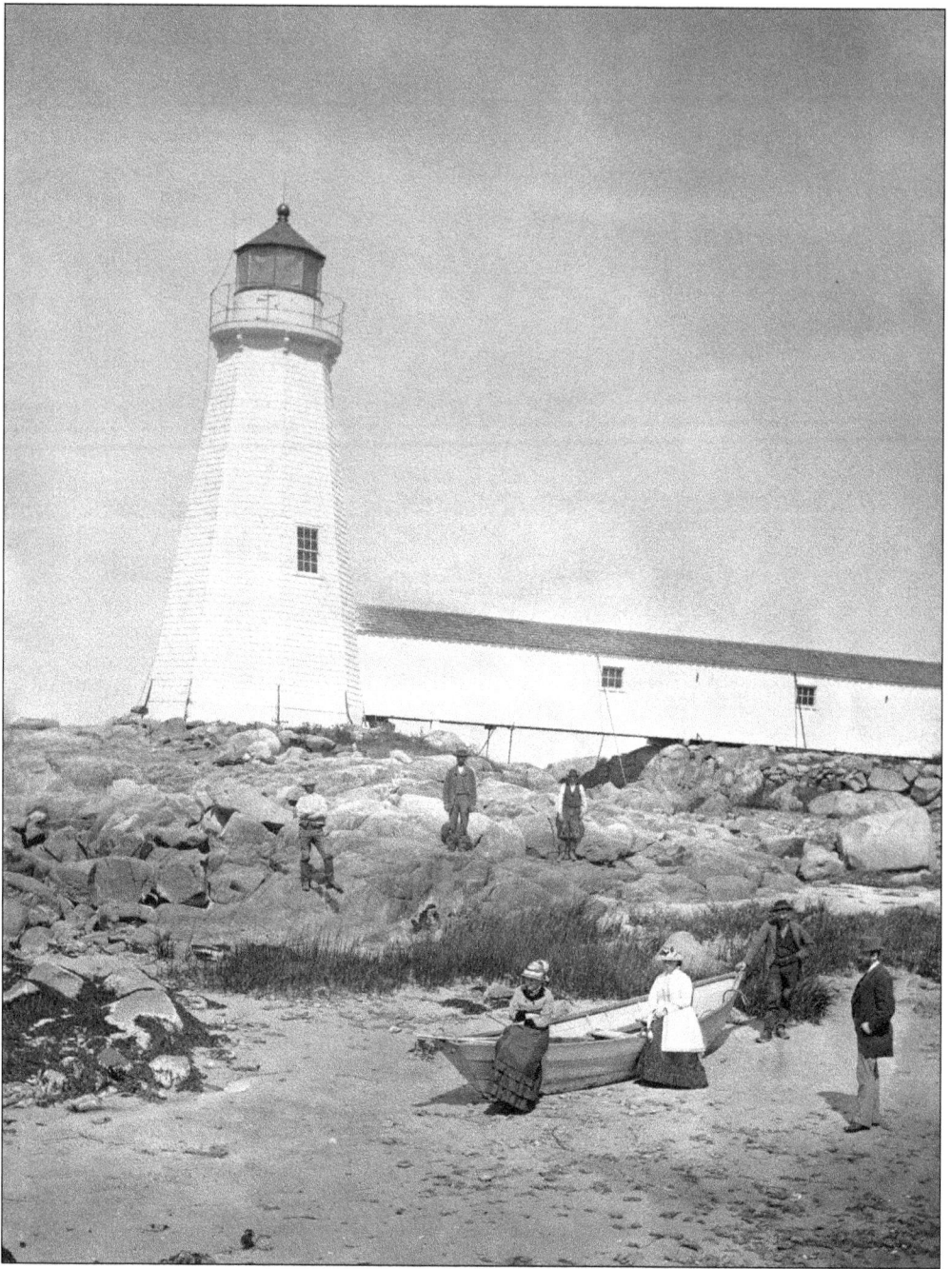

This lighthouse was an essential element for marine navigation, showing the way to the mouth of the river for fishermen who needed to duck in during storms. The river also served as a shortcut to Gloucester Harbor, saving a trip around the cape. The new tower, built in 1851, was a 40-foot octagonal wooden tower that maintained the existing keeper dwelling. The new keeper was William Dade. A fifth-order Fresnel lens rotated by a clockwork mechanism replaced the original reflector Argand lamps around 1857. (CAM.)

This 1880s photograph shows the temporary skeleton tower erected before the new one was completed in 1897. In 1867, the Lighthouse Board reported that a covered walkway from the dwelling to the tower had been built and that other improvements had been made. (CAM.)

This is the original keeper's house before additions were made with the 1851 octagonal tower. The 109-foot covered walkway was added in 1867 and remained in place until 1900. The lifesaving station boathouse is also evident here. (CAM.)

The current tower, built in 1897, includes elements of the original light station complex, such as the keeper's house and an oil house. An elevated covered wooden walkway leads to the 41-foot-tall cylindrical tower, which rests on a stone foundation. The covered walkway was removed in 1900. The lighthouse warns mariners of dangerous obstacles, including long sandbars and a rocky shore along the Annisquam River. (USCG.)

The Massachusetts Humane Society kept a lifeboat in the boathouse at right. The craft proved to be instrumental in saving the life of the crew of the *Abbie B. Cramer*, a three-masted coal schooner from Baltimore that went ashore at the west end of Coffin's Beach, across the river from the lighthouse. The crew of the Davis Neck Lifesaving Station saved the mariners by carrying the lifeboat two miles to the beach near the wreck. (CAM.)

The tower contains a circular cast-iron staircase, made up of 33 steps, that ascends to the watch room. The handrail is wood and possibly hand-cut. An iron ladder leads from the watch room to the lantern room. The wood-frame, two-story building is topped with a gable roof, and it currently serves as US Coast Guard housing. The light station, owned by the Coast Guard, is still an active aid to navigation and is closed to the public. (CAM.)

The schooner *Mexican*, built in Searsport, Maine, in 1833, was considered the fastest topsail schooner in Penobscot Bay. She was a Bangor-to-Boston packet, carrying freight and first-class passengers on a regular schedule. The schooner was lost on Squam Bar in a September nor'easter in 1890, going ashore about 150 yards north of the lighthouse. Laden with coal, she was a total loss. The people of Squam saved on their coal bill that year, salvaging the cargo when it came ashore. (CAM.)

Dennison Hooper served as keeper for 22 years, from 1872 to 1894. His son Edward was born at the lighthouse in 1879. A statement from Dennison's personal diaries reads, "December 18, 1923, I am 82 years old today. I jammed up a bushel of apples and pressed them out. I have made 16 gal. of cider so far. Oats is 9 cents a bag." (CAM.)

John Davis was keeper from 1900 to 1936. Telephone service came, as did city water, in 1907. A more powerful fourth-order Fresnel lens replaced the old fifth-order in 1922 and operated on electricity. This light can be seen up to 15 nautical miles. (SBHS.)

A foghorn was installed in 1931, but it only operated from October to May, in deference to the summer residents' complaints. In the 1950s, the fixed light was changed to a flashing light. A hand-wound mechanism rotated the lens. (CAM.)

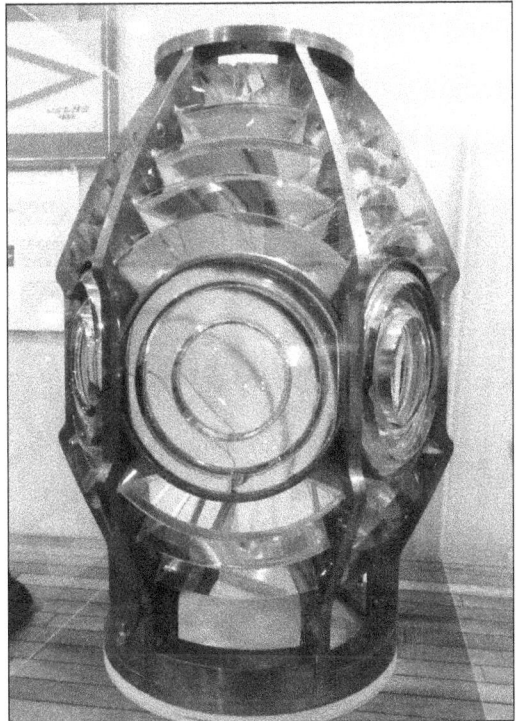

This is the fourth-order Fresnel lens that was housed in the Annisquam light tower for over 50 years. It had replaced the original fifth-order lens in 1922, but the revolving mechanism for the light still had to be wound by hand into the 1950s. (Author's collection.)

Set of 4th Order Lamps. Consisting of 1 Stand and 3 Lamps. The Height of Flame Above Base is Regulated by Height of Stand. The Stand is to be Permanently Fastened Inside the Lens.

These are examples of the oil lamps used in the fourth-order lens. Keepers had to fill them every four hours and clean the lens and lantern room glass of soot. Each lamp sat on a stand like the one at center. Kerosene was delivered in five-gallon cans covered with wood. Lime was delivered in barrels to be used to whitewash the tower. (James W. Claflin for Kenrick A. Claflin & Son.)

The famous sloop *Spray* was a regular visitor in Annisquam in the 1900s following the around-the-world tour undertaken by its captain, Joshua Slocum. He often sailed up and down the Northeast coast during the summer, giving lectures and selling and promoting his book. Here, he sails just in front of the Annisquam Yacht Club. (CAM.)

Edward Hopper, a 20th-century realist artist and one of the giants of American painting, spent the summer of 1912 in Annisquam. He loved painting lighthouses, having done dozens around Gloucester, Ogunquit, and Monhegan Island, Maine, and in Annisquam. This oil painting, *Squam Light*, was produced in 1912. Hopper returned to Gloucester in 1923 and 1924 and began painting watercolors. (CAM.)

This 1960s photograph shows the need for a new paint job on the tower. Also note the fog signal at the lower left of the tower. Some repainting of the tower was done in 1985, and rusted-out iron beams that held up the interior landing below the lantern room were replaced by the late 1990s. (Massachusetts Historical Commission.)

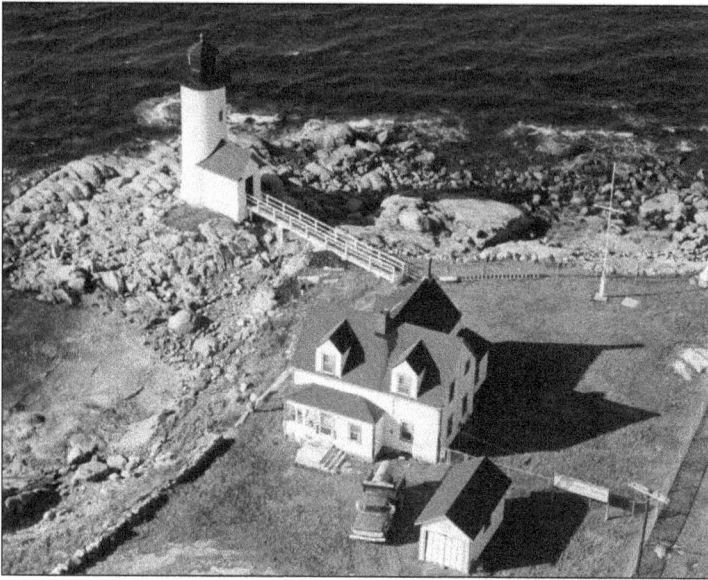

This 1960 aerial photograph of the property shows the keeper's house, garage, and a much more simplified layout following the removal of many of the outbuildings. By 1974, Annisquam Lighthouse was totally automated and keepers were no longer required. After a severe blizzard in 1978, the walkway had to be rebuilt. (USCG.)

In this photograph of the Annisquam Lighthouse, the entry house is seen at center. A new stainless steel door was installed and the wooden walkway and the lighthouse were fully restored in 2000. This view looks across to Wingaersheek Beach, Ipswich Bay, and the mouth of the Annisquam River. The new foghorn, now on its own base, is to the lower right of the tower. (Author's collection.)

Five

STRAITSMOUTH LIGHT STATION
"THE COVE"

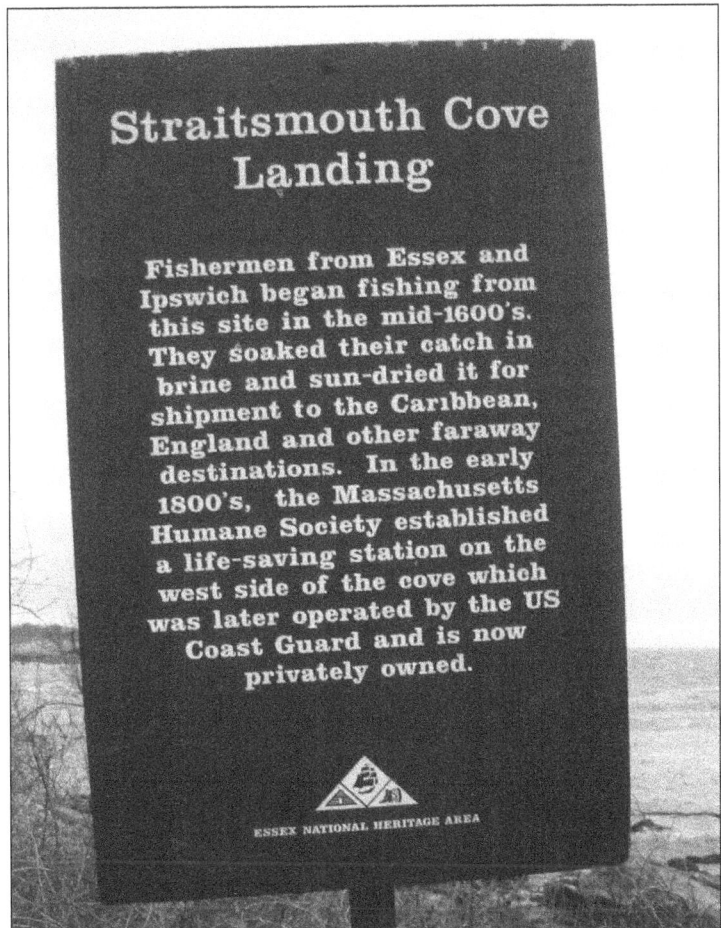

James Babson, one of Cape Ann's original settlers, and his oldest son, John, established the first "stages" (wooden fishing piers) at Straitsmouth Cove in 1690. The lifesaving station was established there in 1889. (Author's collection.)

Straitsmouth Cove Landing

Fishermen from Essex and Ipswich began fishing from this site in the mid-1600's. They soaked their catch in brine and sun-dried it for shipment to the Caribbean, England and other faraway destinations. In the early 1800's, the Massachusetts Humane Society established a life-saving station on the west side of the cove which was later operated by the US Coast Guard and is now privately owned.

ESSEX NATIONAL HERITAGE AREA

Straitsmouth Light, Rockport, Mass.

The first Straitsmouth light was built in 1835, spurred on by the increasing number of ships sailing with cargoes of granite as Rockport's granite industry boomed. Congress approved $5,000 for a lighthouse to help vessels pass through the channel between Thacher Island and the Dry Salvages reef. On November 27, 1834, the island was sold by Aaron and Solomon Poole of Gloucester to the US government for $600. (Robert Ambrogi collection.)

The first lighthouse was only 19 feet tall and poorly constructed, leaky, and with lamps out of plumb. Benjamin Andrews, the first keeper, served until his death in August 1840 at age 58. Ned's Point Light in Mattapoisett, Massachusetts, shown here, was similar in construction and built around the same time, using rubble stone and wood. (Author's collection.)

The 29 acres of Straitsmouth is surrounded by reefs, shoals, and ledges that can be lethal. The lighthouse that stands on the island today is in fact the third to have been built there. Adjacent to Straitsmouth is Avery's Ledge, where Anthony Thacher lost his family. He eventually wound up wrecked on nearby Thacher Island in 1635. (Author's collection.)

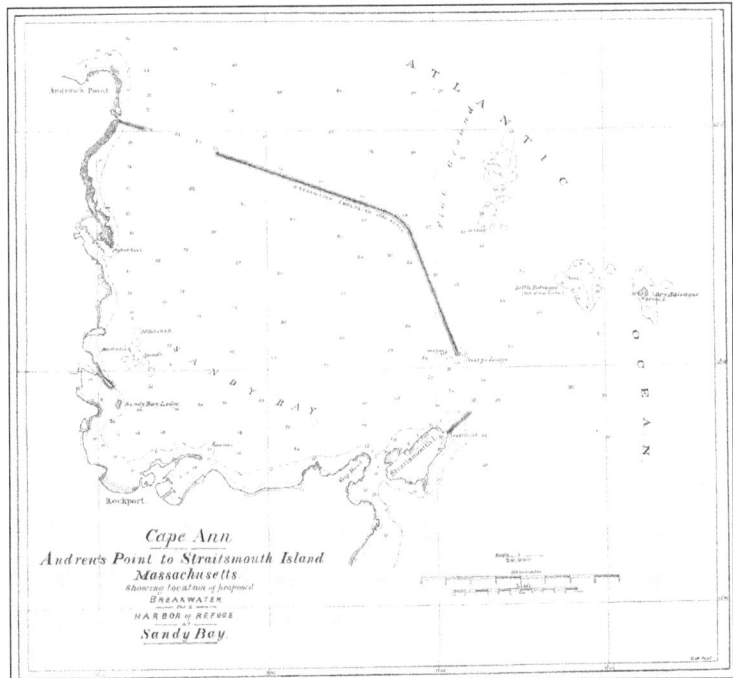

The Sandy Bay National Harbor of Refuge breakwater project was begun on November 12, 1885. A giant 1,600-acre, V-shaped area enclosed by a one-and-a-half-mile granite breakwater was to be erected, with the capacity to hold 5,000 ships. Over a period of 13 years, federal appropriations for the project totaled $5 million. (Author's collection.)

The tug *Confidence* assists the lighter *William H. Moody* place 25-ton decking blocks, which were pinned with two-inch iron rods. The project was eventually abandoned in 1915, having deposited over two million tons of Rockport granite. Only a third of the breakwater was completed. (SBHS.)

The US Navy North Atlantic Fleet came to Sandy Bay harbor, anchoring off of Straitsmouth for many years during summer exercises to help publicize this national project. Today, the breakwater is a hazard to vessels traveling near Straitsmouth and Rockport Harbor. (SBHS.)

AMERICAN CUP DEFENDERS "WEETAMOE" AND "VANITIE" STARTING AT STRAITSMOUTH POINT ON A RACE FROM ROCKPORT, MASS. TO MARBLEHEAD

America's Cup racers sailing past Straitsmouth are depicted in this 1900s postcard. In preparation for the cup in 1934, *Weetamoe* and *Vanitie* sailed a series of races along the New England coast. The last race of the series ran from Rockport to Marblehead on July 9, 1932. *Weetamoe* beat *Vanitie* by 14 minutes to win the series. (Robert Ambrogi collection.)

An 1894 issue of *New England* magazine stated that 147 wrecks and 560 partial disasters were reported in the area in a 20-year period. Here, the schooners *Annie Lee* and *Chilion* are fetched up near Pigeon Cove in 1898 after the "Great Portland Storm." (SBHS.)

Because the first lighthouse was situated 500 feet too far from the point of the island it was intended to warn against, a new one was ordered. In 1851, construction began on the 24-foot-tall octagonal stone tower shown here at a location 87 yards closer to the island's point. (USCG.)

A fixed sixth-order Fresnel lens was added in 1857. It eventually was changed to a beacon with a six-second white blinking light. Henry F. Low of Rockport was appointed the keeper on August 2, 1849. The longest-serving keeper was Nehemiah Knowlton, who lived at the lighthouse for 14 years between 1893 and 1912. (SBHS.)

By 1896, the light again needed rebuilding. This notice to mariners announced the new light and its new location. "Notice is hereby given that, on or about July 30, 1896, the sixth-order fixed white light at this station . . . will be moved . . . to the new tower." (National Archives and Records Administration.)

297.

NOTICE TO MARINERS.

(No. 111 of 1896.)

UNITED STATES OF AMERICA—MASSACHUSETTS.

STRAITSMOUTH LIGHT STATION.

Notice is hereby given that, on or about July 30, 1896, the sixth-order fixed white light at this station, on the N.E. point of Straitsmouth Island, N. side of Cape Ann, will be moved to and exhibited from the new tower recently erected 45 feet N. ⅞ W. from the present temporary tower.

Neither the height of the light above sea level nor its characteristic will be changed.

The new tower is built on the site of the old one, center over center, and is of the same form and color as the old one.

This Notice affects the LIST OF LIGHTS AND FOG SIGNALS, ATLANTIC AND GULF COASTS, 1896, *page* 28, *No.* 84, *and the* LIST OF BEACONS AND BUOYS, SECOND LIGHT-HOUSE DISTRICT, 1895, *pages* 8 *and* 17.

(L. H. B. Notice to Mariners No. 64 of 1896, and Bulletin No. 61, par. 6.)

By order of the Light-House Board:

JOHN G. WALKER,
Rear Admiral, U. S. Navy,
Chairman.

The 37-foot cylindrical brick tower was erected center on center of the original foundation of the 1851 lighthouse. This 1896 lighthouse is the one that stands on Straitsmouth today. (USCG.)

An interesting panorama photograph from 1906 shows the Straitsmouth structures and Thacher Island in the background. In 1867, a boat slip and a 315-foot wooden walkway were added. Note the small structure to the left of the keeper's house, the oil house, which was added in 1905. (SBHS.)

John Cook, seen here with his wife, Emma, and son Donald, was transferred from Thacher Island on February 1, 1918, and served on Straitsmouth until 1925. In 1915, the US Coast Guard was formed and took over Straitsmouth from the US Lighthouse Service, which was absorbed into the Coast Guard in 1939. In 1934, the Coast Guard moved off Straitsmouth to Gap Head Lifesaving Station, a half-mile west on the mainland. (David Cook.)

The current keeper's house was built in 1878. It contained five rooms: two bedrooms, a parlor, a kitchen, and a dining room. It had a covered cistern as well as a milking barn for cows and an outdoor privy. A drainpipe ran from the roof gutter and diverted rainwater into the cistern. The property was valued at $8,100 in 1930, according to the Coast Guard's annual report. That same year, the light was automated. In 1932, the light was changed from white to green, and it has remained that color to the present day. In 1934, the Coast Guard moved off the island, and the government licensed Edward Knowlton to use and occupy the station for $20 per month. The government declared the station surplus in 1937 and disposed of it. (SBHS.)

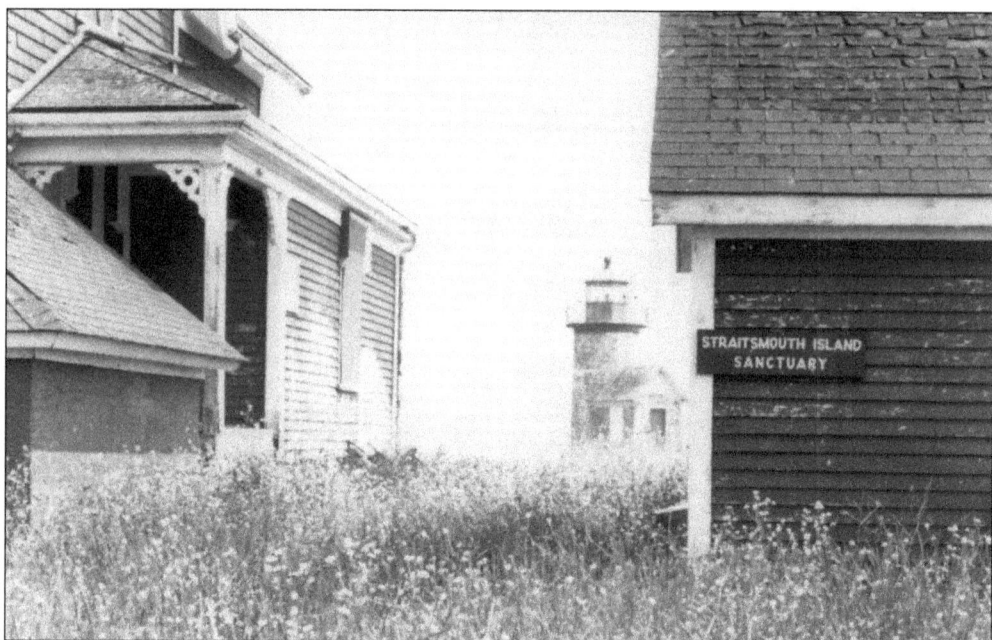

In this 1967 photograph, the house (left) is already beginning to deteriorate. It was totally abandoned by 1970 and turned into a wildlife sanctuary. This view from the backyard shows the barn (right), the covered cistern (far left), and the tower. (Massachusetts Historical Commission.)

The eastern wall of the keeper's house collapsed in 2010. The Massachusetts Audubon Society has recently stabilized the structure with a new roof, clapboards, and windows. (Author's collection.)

OLD "CAPE ANN SLOOP" SAILING THROUGH THE "GAP" BETWEEN STRAITSMOUTH AND "GAPHEAD" ROCKPORT, MASS.

This Charles Cleaves photograph shows the boathouse to the right of the sloop on the west end of the island. A granite sloop passes through the Gap on its way to Pigeon Cove. The photograph was used in a postcard in 1925. (SBHS.)

Straitsmouth Island has gone through many ownership changes over the years. In 1941, it was sold to Glenn Wilson of New York City for $3,050. Wilson was a playwright and an advertising copywriter. The island was purchased in the late 1940s by Edward Nelson Wendell, who also owned property on Bearskin Neck in Rockport. (SBHS.)

William Francis Gibbs bought the island in the mid-1950s. Gibbs, a famous naval architect and marine engineer, directed the design and production of Liberty ships in World War II and designed the SS *United States* luxury liner. On her maiden voyage on July 4, 1952, she broke *Queen Mary's* 14-year-old transatlantic record by 10 hours. Gibbs never lived on the island but built a home that had a view of it from the living room. (SBHS.)

When Gibbs died in 1967, his brother Frederick gave the island to the Massachusetts Audubon Society. A plaque on a giant boulder on the island marks the occasion. (Author's collection.)

Straitsmouth Lighthouse was automated with solar power for both the light and the fog signal in 1990. In this photograph, the solar panels can be seen on the tower parapet railing. In October 1991, the area was hit by the No-Name Storm, sometimes referred to as the "Perfect Storm," which completely destroyed the entry house. The Coast Guard repaired it in 1992–1993 and decided not to replace the entry room cabin. (Author's collection.)

In 2000, the National Lighthouse Preservation Act was passed, which allowed the US Coast Guard to offer its lighthouse inventory to interested parties who would agree to maintain them as historic landmarks. The Thacher Island Association and the Town of Rockport accepted ownership of the tower and 1.8 acres of land from the National Park Service, the General Services Administration, and the US Coast Guard in 2011. (Author's collection.)

Unfortunately, Straitsmouth is still claiming victims. Local fisherman Capt. Bill Lee lost his fishing dragger *Ocean Reporter* in October 2011. The Coast Guard and harbormasters were unable to pull it off the ledge. The tide was going, and by 7:00 the next morning, the vessel had turned over and went under. The tight-knit community of Rockport came together and raised enough money for Lee to replace his boat. (Author's collection.)

Straitsmouth Light Station is listed in the National Register of Historic Places, one of only 10 structures in Rockport. It joins the National Historic Landmark of Thacher Island Lighthouse Station as a cultural and historic icon to be enjoyed by the public for years to come. (Author's collection.)

72

Six

CAPE ANN LIGHT STATION
"THACHER'S WOE"

Thacher Island is located on the eastern shore of Rockport, Massachusetts, a half-mile offshore and about three miles from Rockport Harbor. Milk Island is located to the south, Straitsmouth Island to the northwest, the Londoner reef to the east, and Dry and Little Salvages reefs to the north. The island is approximately 52 acres. In 2002, the US Coast Guard gave the southern 29 acres of the island to the Town of Rockport. The northern 22 acres are owned by the US Fish & Wildlife Service, which also owns the North Tower. (TIA.)

Anthony Thacher and his family were sailing from Ipswich to Marblehead when a violent storm appeared and sank their pinnace, a two-masted boat used for fishing. Only Anthony and his wife, Elizabeth, survived. Among the 21 fatalities were the following: the crew; Thacher's cousin Rev. John Avery and his family; and Thacher's four children. The island was later named after Anthony Thacher. He was awarded 40 marks by the General Court of Massachusetts "towards

his great losses." In 1636, Gov. John Winthrop and the court granted Thacher "the small island at the head of Cape Ann, upon which he was preserved from shipwreck as his proper inheritance." The island was subsequently sold in 1714 to Rev. John White of Gloucester, who paid 100 pounds. In a letter to his brother Peter in England recounting the tragedy, Thacher called the island "Thacher's Woe, which I named after my name." (CAM.)

The island has changed dramatically since Anthony Thacher's wreck in 1635. It is dominated by a number of buildings erected since 1771. Today, the island has 10 structures, including the twin lighthouses, two keeper dwellings, a whistle house (fog signal), oil house, boathouse and ramp, cistern, utility house, railway, campground, helicopter pad, and about three miles of walking trails. (USCG.)

The first lighthouse towers on Thacher Island were built in 1771 by the Massachusetts Bay Colony under British rule. John Hancock, who had significant shipping interests in the area, presented his petition to the General Court and proposed to tax Boston ship owners for "light money" to cover the costs of building and maintaining the lighthouses. (CAM.)

Two new towers and a brick keeper dwelling were built in 1861. The South Tower is shown here, along with the covered walkway and the fog signal building. Ironically, Rockport, known for its many granite quarries, did not supply the stone for these towers. As a result of political pressure, New Hampshire granite was used instead. The towers' location on Cape Ann spawned the nickname "Anne's Eyes" by the locals. (National Archives and Records Administration.)

"Why two lighthouses?" Lighthouses today have distinctive flashing patterns known as "characteristics" that enable mariners to differentiate one tower from another. In an earlier time, however, flashing technology was unavailable. In order to distinguish Thacher Light from Boston Light, 24 miles to the south, and Portsmouth Light, 30 miles to the north, two lighthouses were built. Standing 300 yards apart, they mark the boundaries of the Londoner reef about a half-mile off the island. (CAM.)

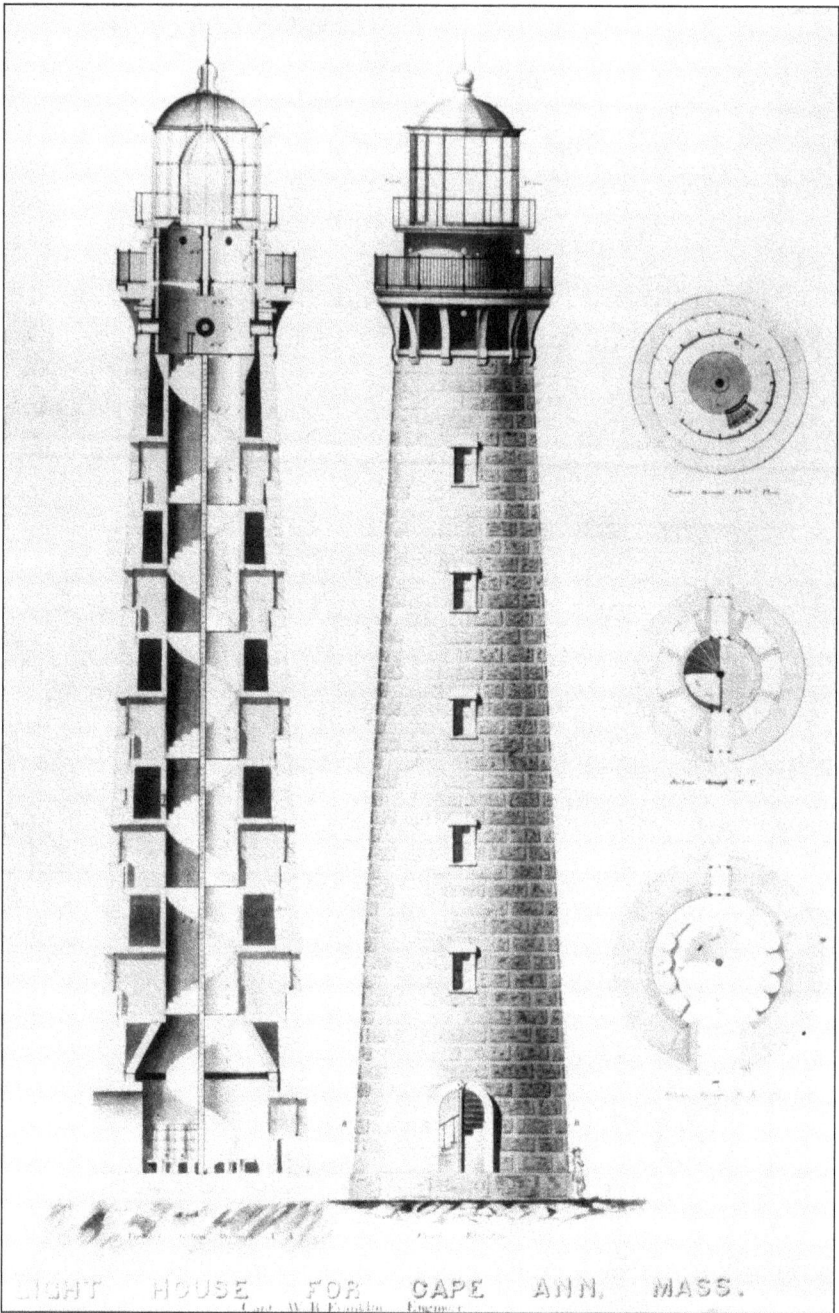

These are the original construction drawings for the Cape Ann lighthouses. Each tower stands 124 feet tall and 160 feet above mean high tide, is 30 feet in diameter at the base, and is 18 feet in diameter at the lantern. There are five decks in the 156-step spiral staircase. Five slit windows each appear on the east and west sides, providing light to the staircase. Two stages of balconies encircle the upper tower. The granite exterior is separated from the brick-lined interior wall by a space of 18 inches. Each block of granite was precut, numbered, and fitted on shore, and a team of oxen moved the blocks to a granite sloop that brought them to the work site on the island. The walls of the towers are four to five feet thick. (National Archives and Records Administration.)

A first-order Fresnel lens (the largest of the seven orders or sizes) was installed in each tower in 1861. The principal of light refraction was used to form a single concentrated shaft of light traveling in one direction, making each light visible from 22 miles away. Each light weighs over a ton, stands 10 feet high and 6 feet in diameter, and is made up of over 400 crystal glass prisms mounted in a bronze framework. When this lens was electrified in 1932, it was reported in the July 1 edition of the *Lighthouse Service Bulletin* that "the master of the steamship *Falmouth* has reported seeing the new light at Cape Ann, Mass, a distance of 44 miles." This observation was made on the night of May 3, 1932. The lens shown here was removed from the South Tower in 1980 and is now displayed as shown at the Cape Ann Museum in Gloucester in 2013. (TIA.)

This original lamp is on display in the Thacher Museum. Whale or sperm oil was discontinued in 1850 due to its cost and scarcity. Lard oil was substituted until the 1870s, when kerosene, known as "mineral oil," became the illuminant. The lamp used a five-ring wick. An early Lighthouse Service Annual Report noted that a typical first-order lamp, such as this one, burned 2,282 gallons of oil a year. (TIA.)

The North Tower, which is an exact duplicate of the South Tower, stands on a high promontory on the northern end of the island. It was attended to by keepers who lived in the dwelling shown here at lower right. The tower stands 112 feet tall to the focal point of the light, and 166 feet above the mean high tide mark. When first electrified, it used four 250-watt bulbs surrounded by the huge Fresnel lens, which magnified the light to 70,000 candlepower. Lights had to be checked every four hours. (National Archives and Records Administration.)

This three-story duplex, built in 1861, housed two keeper families, living one above the other. It replaced the first keeper's house. The contract for the new house, dated October 10, 1810, was "to build a stone dwelling house for use of the keeper on Thatcher [sic] Island Lighthouse thirty four feet long and twenty feet wide, one story of eight feet high, divided into two rooms sixteen feet by twelve each." (National Archives and Records Administration.)

In 1932, Pres. Franklin Roosevelt shut down the North Tower lighthouse as a cost-saving measure during the Depression. This photograph reveals that the roof of the entry room has gone missing after the tower was abandoned around 1940. (Massachusetts Historical Commission.)

The North Tower keeper dwelling, built in 1869, housed two families. Originally, it had one kitchen, on the west side; a second kitchen was added to the east side around 1889. Covered walkways were helpful in winter snowstorms and summer rains, as keepers were required to tend the lights every four hours during the night in the early years. Over time, as lights required less tending due to electric power, the covered walkway was removed. A third keeper dwelling was built in 1874 for the principal keeper and his family. The building cost was $2,503.47, according to the Lighthouse Board records of May 26, 1875. The two remaining keeper's houses were restored in 2004–2008. A visitor center and museum are free to the public. A reproduction of a Victorian-era parlor with period furniture, including a pump organ, illustrates how the keepers lived in the 1890s. (CAM.)

HARPER'S WEEKLY.

JOURNAL OF CIVILIZATION

NEW YORK, SATURDAY, DECEMBER 30, 1876.

Keepers had to climb the 156 steps in each tower every four hours during the night to trim the wicks, clean the lens and glass, and add more oil to the lamp. In addition, they had to manage the steam-powered engine (for the foghorn) in the whistle house. This illustration from the December 30, 1876, edition of *Harper's Weekly* shows the keeper chipping ice off the lantern-room glass at Christmastime. There were 23 principal lighthouse keepers on Thacher Island between 1771 and 1939, when the US Coast Guard took over. There were more than 150 assistants stationed there as well. Many keepers were veterans of the Revolutionary War, Civil War, or the Spanish-American War. Some keepers were former seamen or had been in the marine trades. In the early 1800s, most keepers were political patronage choices based on the administration in power at the time. (TIA.)

Alexander Bray was principal keeper in 1864. Three days before Christmas, he took his assistant to the doctor in Rockport. A severe snowstorm blew in, preventing his return. During his absence, his wife, Maria, and her nephew, Sidney Haskell, were forced to walk the 300 yards between each light, through huge snow drifts and gale-force winds, and climb each tower's 156 steps three times each night to trim the wicks, refill the oil lamps, and clean the lens. Because the lights were kept aflame, Alexander was finally able to return with his assistant on Christmas Eve. USCGC *Maria Bray* was named in Maria's honor in 2000. The vessel, the 12th cutter of the Keeper class of coastal buoy tenders, is 175 feet long and has a crew of one officer and 17 enlisted. She was commissioned in Mayport, Florida, on July 26, 2000. (TIA.)

William Daggett (1870–1945) was first assistant keeper from 1918 to 1926. He raised cows and sheep on the island. Prior to joining the Lighthouse Service, he was a cook aboard the "rock" sloop *America* at age 14, delivering granite up and down the Eastern Seaboard. He later became a mate and pilot on the tug *H.S. Nichols*, working for the Rockport Granite Company for 28 years. (TIA.)

Felix Doyle worked for head keeper Alexander Bray from July 8, 1865, to April 5, 1866, as first assistant. He was paid $300 per year. Doyle was later transferred to Plum Island Light and served there until 1882. He enrolled in the Army on July 10, 1861, and was assigned to the 19th Regiment, Massachusetts Volunteer Infantry in Company G in Washington, DC. Doyle was mustered out as a corporal on July 22, 1864. (Edward J. Everett.)

Unidentified keepers pose on the back porch of the principal keeper's house on July 28, 1896. The ship's wheel was salvaged from a shipwreck. The keepers at that time were James Allison, E.C. Hadley, Frank Hall, and Albert Whitten. Whitten, in the North Tower, was the last person to see the ill-fated SS *Portland*, about a mile off Thacher, before she sank in 1898. On August 24, 1893, the 25-year-old Whitten and assistant E.C. Hadley risked their lives to save the four-man crew of the *Lottie B*, a schooner from St. John, New Brunswick, that struck the Londoner and came ashore on Thacher. She had struck in the fog at 4:00 a.m., floated free of the ledge, and anchored to await assistance. Meanwhile, the wind increased, endangering the crew, the ship, and the cargo of lumber. At 10:00 a.m., the tug *Cornelia* and the Massachusetts Humane Society's boats had arrived on the scene, but they were too late to help. The *Lottie B* dragged her anchor, drifted on the rocks, and crashed to pieces, her cargo of lumber drifting away while Whitten and Hadley made their dramatic rescue. Both received the Massachusetts Humane Society's gold plaque for heroism. (TIA.)

This c. 1873 photograph shows two fog signal buildings next to the South Tower. Mariners complained that the horn could not be heard, and it was declared inefficient by the Lighthouse Service in 1866. The second house, built closer to the tower, had a 32-inch Ericsson steam engine and a 15-foot horn erected on the roof. (National Archives and Records Administration.)

By 1874, the second horn also proved to be ineffectual, and it was replaced with a 10-inch steam whistle in 1887. The fog signal house shown here is the current 32-foot-square brick building. It was erected for $2,200 and approved by the Lighthouse Board on October 7, 1886. The building became known as the "Whistle House." (National Archives and Records Administration.)

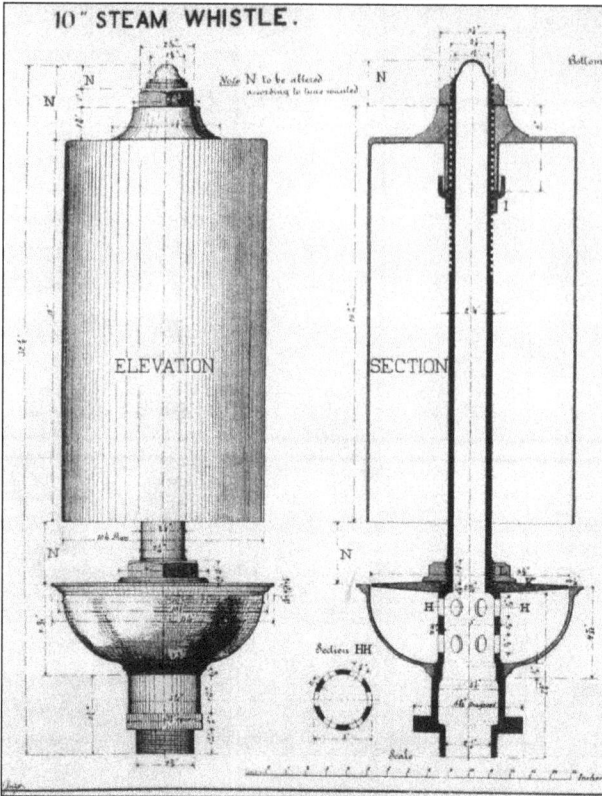

10" STEAM WHISTLE.

ELEVATION   SECTION

This drawing from the 1901 US Lighthouse Service supply depot catalog of standard articles shows the type of whistle used at Thacher. It was a 10-inch steam-powered brass train whistle able to be heard for five miles in foggy weather. The catalog price in 1901 was $35. (James W. Claflin collection.)

This photograph shows the Whistle House with its tall brick chimney. Next to it is the 6,000-gallon, triangular-roofed covered cistern, which stored water for the Crosby steam engine. It was built in 1900. The tramway trestle, which climbs to the roof of the Whistle House, allows coal carts to dump their load into the coal bin dormer. The signal characteristic was an eight-second blast, a four-second silence, a four-second blast, and a 44-second silence. (TIA.)

The lighthouse tender *Mayflower* was used by the 2nd Coast Guard District from 1898 to 1924 to deliver supplies to Thacher Island. Tenders also carried library books in wooden cases that were exchanged by keepers among different light stations. Lighthouse tenders were named after trees and flowers. Other tenders that serviced Cape Ann Light Station were *Daisy* (1877–1879), *Fern* (1884), *Verbena* (1875–1889), *Geranium* (1889), *Myrtle* (1902), *Ameria* (1903), *Azalea* (1919–1926), and *Lotus* (1926). (USCG.)

This c. 1948 photograph shows the tramway running from the boathouse (not shown to the left) to the Whistle House (not shown to the right). The turntable in the center allows tramway carts to be sent in any direction. Keepers had to unload as much as 30 tons of coal at a time from the tenders. The coal then had to be hauled across the island to the Whistle House via carts. This tramway has recently been rebuilt by the Thacher Island Association volunteers. (USCG.)

The first boathouse and ramp were built in 1842 under the direction of keeper Charles Wheeler. Since then, the structures have been replaced at least six times due to severe storms. Note the railway tracks to the right of the ramp that allowed the cart to go to the water's edge to receive materials from the lighthouse tender. (TIA.)

3957—TWIN LIGHTS, THATCHER'S ISLAND, OFF BASS ROCKS, GLOUCESTER, MASS.

Cape Ann Light Station at Thacher Island was designated a National Historic Landmark in 2001, one of only 10 lighthouse stations to be so designated as of 2009. The twin lighthouses of Thacher were the first to mark a "dangerous spot in the ocean," whereas all previous lights had been erected to mark harbor entrances. (TIA.)

Seven

GAP COVE
LIFESAVING STATION
"THE GAP"

In 1785, the Massachusetts Humane Society initiated the world's first organized lifesaving service. It established 92 huts of refuge around the Massachusetts coastline, providing shelter and food for shipwreck survivors. Shown here is the hut in Marblehead, designated as No. 10 of the 92. The society had huts of refuge, boathouses, and mortar stations (from which mortars were used to fire lines to stricken ships at sea). (James Claflin collection.)

In 1872, the US government established the US Life Saving Service. Eventually, 280 lifesaving stations were built. The Humane Society and the Life Saving Service coexisted but often competed to be the first on the scene of a disaster. In 1869, surfboat stations were reported at Lanesville in Gloucester and at Emerson Point in Rockport, and a mortar station was operated by Jonathan Parsons in Rockport.

In 1880, there were 15 lifesaving stations in the Massachusetts District. Plum Island was designated No. 1, Davis Neck was No. 2, and Gap Cove was No. 3. Others were located in Rockport, on Middle Street on Bear Skin Neck (No. 4), and at Emerson Point (No. 5). Some of the stations were simply boathouses, while others were fully equipped with lifesaving gear. In 1869, a hut of refuge was reported by the Humane Society on Milk Island in Rockport, run by William Stillman. Others were spread along the Massachusetts coast all the way to Cape Cod. (George Grimes.)

Gap Cove Lifesaving Station was established in 1887 as a replacement for the original Davis Neck Station in Annisquam. It was built in the Duluth-style architecture of the time. There were 28 similarly styled stations in the country, six in Massachusetts. (SBHS.)

In 1902, the Gap Cove Lifesaving Station was renamed Straitsmouth Station. This postcard shows a local farmer harvesting seaweed to be used as fertilizer, a process that continued into the 1930s. (SBHS.)

Employees of the Life Saving Service were called "surfmen" and were usually experienced seamen. The crews were made up of six to eight men. Shown here on January 1, 1903, are, from left to right, Capt. C.A. Bearse, George E. Sanders, G.G. Stanwood, Joshua C. Eldridge, Elmer F. Kenrick, John E. Parsons, G.E. Prankard, and E.B. Haskell. (George Grimes.)

A lifesaving crew poses for a photograph around 1903. The surfboats were wheeled on a beach cart to the rocky shore of the Gap. George Grimes's grandfather was stationed here in 1915. These are photographs from his book *Water Under the Keel*, published in 2011. Note the old Straitsmouth Inn in the background at upper left. (George Grimes.)

94

Among the beach apparatus shown here are the throwing lines and a Lyle gun. The gun was used to fire the line to a sinking ship, thus setting up the breeches buoy to get the crew off. (George Grimes.)

This pulling surfboat accommodated six men with six oars. These boats were about 25–28 feet long. This crew is shown in the Gap, with Straitsmouth on the right. (George Grimes.)

Around 1917, the Coast Guard started using 30-foot motor surfboats. This photograph, taken on October 23, 1916, shows a surfboat from Point Adams in Oregon on the Columbia River. Seen here are the rudder and the brass propeller. Note the men in their cork life jackets and the railroad tracks that were used to get the heavy surfboat down to the water. (James Claflin collection.)

On February 28, 1902, during a fierce gale, the tramp steamer *Wilster* of West Hartlepool, England, ran aground on a ledge near Thacher Island. It soon came free but then washed ashore on Long Beach in Rockport. The vessel suffered no major structural damage, although leaks broke out in some compartments. All crewmembers made it safely ashore. The *Wilster* was headed for Boston with 1,325 tons of sugar in 200-pound bags. (CAM.)

In short order, barges were dispatched to unload the *Wilster*'s cargo in order to allow a flotilla of six tugs to pull the vessel free of the beach. But bad weather and thick fog delayed salvage efforts, and the *Wilster* became further embedded in the sandy beach, all the while taking on more water. The effort took nearly a month; it was March 22 before the steamer was finally pulled free. (SBHS.)

Not surprisingly, the stranded vessel drew crowds of onlookers from Rockport, Gloucester, and beyond. For a time, some of the crewmembers were put up in nearby Rockport homes and at the lifesaving station at Gap Cove. This event was so newsworthy that a postcard of the stranded steamer was produced five years later, in 1907. Note the Thacher towers in the background. (SBHS.)

In 1915, President Wilson created the US Coast Guard by combining the US Life Saving Service and the US Revenue Cutter Service. By 1939, the US Lighthouse Service was also incorporated into the USCG. The lifesaving station officially became the Straitsmouth US Coast Guard Station No. 22 by 1937. (George Grimes.)

The coastal tanker *Chelsea* left Boston on February 10, 1957, with a load of fuel oil for delivery to Newington, New Hampshire. Visibility was good, but a 35-mile-per-hour northwesterly wind was whipping up seas offshore. Trying to hug the shoreline to take advantage of its protection, the ship grounded off Loblolly Cove a half-mile northeast of Thacher Island. The captain cut too close to the submerged Sandy Bay Breakwater, and the ship sustained an 80-foot gash in her side. (SBHS.)

Capt. Keith Beale (lower right) and the crew of the *Chelsea*, who jumped for their lives, were saved by the Coast Guard cutter *Evergreen* and by a 35-foot motor lifeboat. The *Chelsea* actually freed herself on the tide, but the opened gash from the bow to near amidships caused her to fill with water, and the vessel settled to the bottom off Loblolly Cove. She split in half and today is a prime site for scuba divers. (SBHS.)

On the evening of April 1, 1946, during a blinding snowstorm, the 7,000-ton Liberty ship *Charles S. Haight* was found off of Cape Ann, returning "in ballast" (without cargo) to New York after delivering coal to Newport, England. A strong wind blew the lightened ship onto Flatground reef inside Dry Salvages, off of Straitsmouth Island. The steamer slid high on the ledge and resisted all attempts to free it. (SBHS.)

The punctured hull of the *Charles S. Haight* had filled with water near the No. 5 hold. By noon the next day, the captain and crew were ordered to lifeboats and removed to the Coast Guard cutter *Ojibwa*. The ship broke in two at the No. 4 hold and was a total loss. Her engine block can still be seen at low tide in front of the breakwater. In 1916, the torpedo destroyer USS *Warrington* hit this reef, her propellers were torn off, and the vessel had to be towed to Boston for repairs. (SBHS.)

The Life Saving Servicemen's motto was "You have to go, but you don't have to come back." This often proved true, as many did not come back. The Life Saving Service Annual Report of 1916 stated that 1,216 lives were saved, 15,742 persons were assisted, and 1,453 vessels were assisted. During that year, the estimated value of ships lost was $10,509,655. (George Grimes.)

This postcard has a postmark of June 17, 1912. The two large doors at center housed the surfboats. The building on the far right, called the Humane Building, was probably the original Massachusetts Humane Society hut of refuge from the early 1800s. At one time, horses were kept there. (Robert Ambrogi collection.)

U. S. Life Saving Station, Lands End, Rockport, Mass.

Here is the breeches buoy in action. Note the mast on the left. This was used to simulate a ship's mast at sea as a target for the surfmen to practice shooting the line for the breeches buoy. (SBHS.)

During World War II, a giant radio tower was built, one of three on the property. It was erected by the Raytheon Corporation and was reported to be 156 feet high. The cabin, located about 65 feet up the tower, was used by the watch standers and housed radios and radar equipment. (Author's collection.)

This aerial photograph reveals that the station was in a residential neighborhood. At the top are the Seafarer Inn and Seward Inn. On the right is a private home once owned by the founder of the Thacher Island Association, Ned Cameron. Note the number 22 on the station's lawn, which designated it as USCG Station 22 from the air. (USCG.)

The station was closed in 1964. It was sold to a private individual in 1968 and is now owned by an admiralty lawyer. This is how the station looks today. Over the years, porches were built, rooms were added, and the barn is now an apartment. Note that one of the original flagpole towers still stands. (Author's collection.)

Eight

Davis Neck
Lifesaving Station
"Bay View"

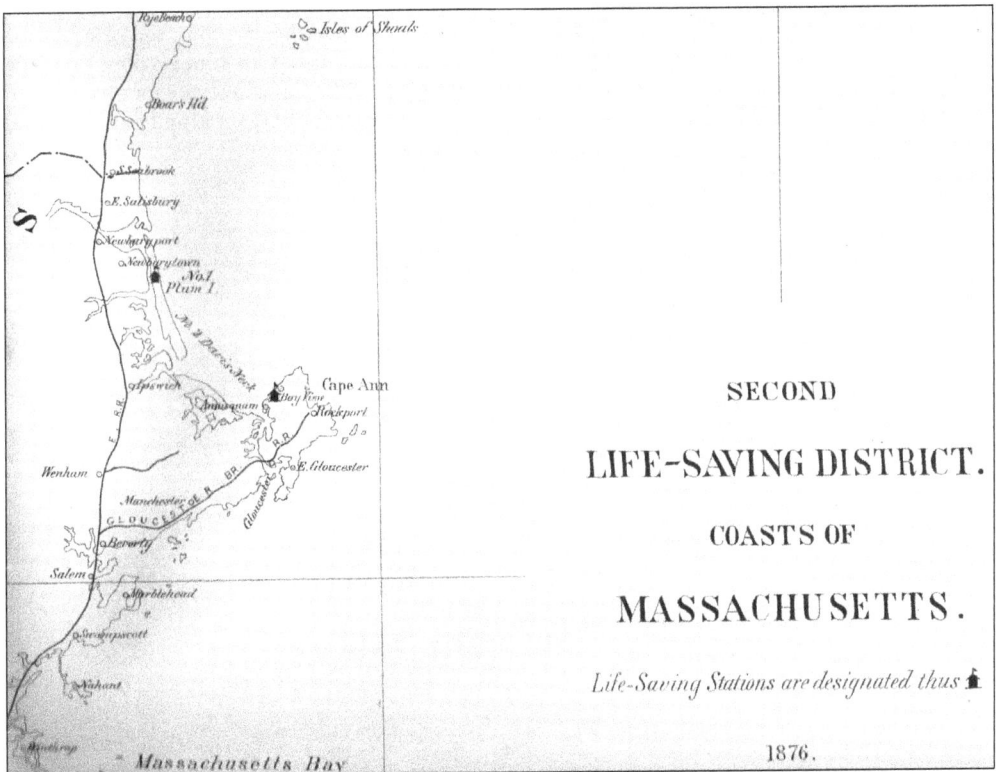

Davis Neck juts into the bay about a half-mile from Wigwam Point and the Annisquam Light Station. A watch house was built there in 1705 to help guard against surprise by French and Indian raiders and to give warning of approaching pirates. This lifesaving station map from 1876 shows the location of Davis Neck Station No. 2, at left, near Bay View and the mouth of the Annisquam River. (Author's collection.)

The Davis Neck Lifesaving Station at Bay View was one of the busiest lookout stations on Cape Ann in the days of sail. Locating the entrance to Lane's Cove in a fog was tricky for any skipper. In 1880, keeper James W. Marchant of Lanesville kept his men busy practicing boat drills and using Lyle guns to shoot lines to "sinking ships" in the bay. (CAM.)

The crew stationed at the Davis Neck Lifesaving Station is seen here on August 16, 1887. They are, from left to right, Jabez Marchant Jr. (keeper), Levi P. Lane, Samuel S. Butler, Horatio Marchant, William Knowlton, Daniel Robinson Jr., and Benjamin Newman. (CAM.)

Following Colonial customs, the crew maintained burning beacons all night long. Its job was to guard not only the dangerous Squam River sandbars but also the rocky coves at Bay View and the entrance to Lane's Cove. The actual station is on the mainland to the right, while Davis Neck itself is the small peninsula on the left. (CAM.)

The Davis Neck crew is seen here around 1885. Shown here are, from left to right, Capt. Jabez Marchant Jr., George Saunders, Ben Tucker, George Stanwood, Francis J. Cook, Leonard G. Day, and Benjamin G. Newman. Note the model of the breeches buoy in the lower right, currently at the Cape Ann Museum. Eventually, this picturesque building became the site of estates owned by Gen. Benjamin Butler and Col. Jonas French, and the Annisquam Lighthouse took over as sentinel in the area. (CAM.)

Lifesaving stations were typically two-story houses made of tongue-and-groove pine, with gable roofs covered with cypress or cedar shingles. The stations were of chalet style, with heavy projecting eaves and a small open observatory on the peaked roof in which a flagstaff stood. They were 25 feet wide by 45 feet long. (Appleton's "Annual Cyclopedia" for 1878.)

By 1883, Davis Neck was abandoned because of its location facing the teeth of every nor'easter. It suffered constant damage. The station was reestablished in a more protected area and moved to Gap Cove Station in Rockport in 1889. Davis Neck was a defense post in both world wars, and machine gun nests from World War II are still seen in the hollows between the ledges on the neck. (Author's collection.)

The ground floor contained two rooms: a boat room, occupying two-thirds of the ground floor, and a general living room for the crew. The second story had three rooms: one for equipment, a keeper's sleeping room, and a room for the men and shipwreck survivors. This station building was converted to a summer cottage by a private resident, who added a porch, railings, and an extra room. (Author's collection.)

The Davis Neck Lifesaving Station was built in 1874 on land owned by Civil War general Benjamin Butler, who owned a 47-acre estate in the Bay View section of Annisquam. General Butler's home, seen here in 1880, looked down to the station on Davis Neck. (CAM.)

This is the home today, occupied by members of the original Ames/Butler family. (Author's collection.)

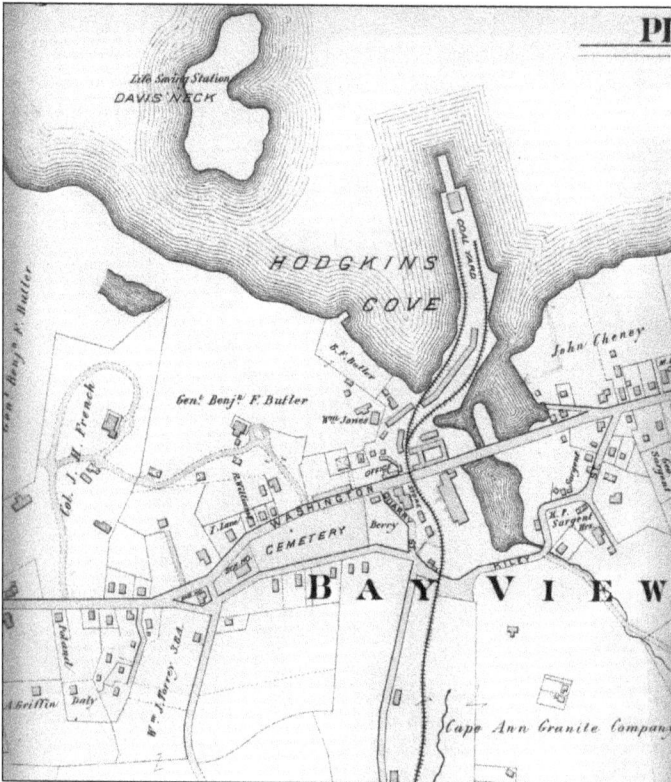

This map shows the location of Davis Neck, near Hodgkin's Cove. Butler's home is indicated on the map, as is that of Col. Jonas French, who partnered with Butler to create the Cape Ann Granite Company. Colonel French was Butler's aide-de-camp when he commanded the 30th Massachusetts Volunteer Infantry Regiment during Butler's controversial administration in 1862 of the captured New Orleans. (SBHS.)

Butler was a soldier, lawyer, politician, and the 33rd governor of Massachusetts. He ran for president in 1884 with the Greenback Party. Butler was a savvy politician but not a great military man. A favorite of Abraham Lincoln, who made him a major general, Butler's failures in battle cost him his job. Ulysses S. Grant had to fire him. Lincoln later asked Butler to be his vice-presidential running mate, but he declined. (Author's collection.)

Butler, a controversial character, was often criticized in the press. He did have some redeeming values, for instance as a staunch defender of civil rights. He introduced the first civil rights bill in the US Congress in 1875. Butler was a friend of labor and championed Irish immigrants. At one point, his reputation was so negative that his picture was placed at the bottom of chamber pots sold across the country. (Author's collection.)

In 1867, Butler formed the Cape Ann Granite Company in his backyard in Bay View. It was co-owned by Col. Jonas French. The quarry provided stone for their homes, which they built on the property. Their quarry also provided stone for post offices in Boston and Baltimore and for the foundation of the Brooklyn Bridge. They built a railroad in 1870 to haul the granite to the company's docks in Lanesville. (CAM.)

In 1873, Butler purchased the yacht *America* from the US Navy, which had been using her as a training ship. She had been used as a racer in 1851 and was the namesake for the famous America's Cup race. Butler sailed her out of Gloucester until his death in 1893. Apparently, Butler wanted the lifesaving station built so that when he sailed the rocky shores near his home, he would have a sense of safety. (CAM.)

William R. Cheves established the Cheves Green Granite Company in Lanesville in 1876. The Cheves quarry was adjacent to the Cape Ann Granite Company quarry. Part of Cheves's holdings included Devil Rock Pit. He is shown here holding a work order. His father had quarried stones for Balmoral Castle in Scotland, and Cheves himself started as a paving-stone cutter. Cheves, while under contract with the Rockport Granite Company, quarried most of the stone for Dog Bar Breakwater during the 11 years of its construction. (CAM.)

Stone carrier *Jonas H. French* is shown here in Lane's Cove in winter ice. The vessel is picking up paving stones. Granite sloops plied the waters around Cape Ann and traveled all the way to New York, New Orleans, and the Caribbean. Cape Ann Granite Company was the largest supplier of paving stones in the nation. The industry lasted until the 1930s, when the call for granite paving blocks was reduced as asphalt and cement roadways became the norm. (CAM.)

Lane's Cove is seen here in 1869 with fish sheds and dories in the background. Fishermen salted their catch in the sheds before the products were shipped to Boston. As the stone business grew, it became necessary to build a huge breakwater for shelter from heavy storms. It can be seen in the left background. A toll was charged to all vessels and fishing boats for the use of the piers. Most granite was shipped by water to Boston, New York, and Philadelphia. (SBHS.)

Joshua Slocum's 36-foot, gaff-rigged oyster sloop *Spray* is tied up at the pier at Lane's Cove Granite Company at low tide. Paving stones are stacked on the pier. Slocum was the first man to sail around the world alone, from 1895 to 1898. His book, *Sailing Alone Around the World*, was an international best seller in 1900. He disappeared in November 1909 while sailing to the West Indies, where he wintered each year. (CAM.)

Pigeon Cove in Rockport was connected to the quarry system across Cape Ann via a rail system. The Rockport Granite Company bought out the bankrupted Cape Ann Granite Company in 1893. (SBHS.)

The three-masted granite ship *William D. May* arrives in Pigeon Cove to pick up paving blocks destined for Philadelphia city streets. (SBHS.)

This arch bridge was built on Granite Street in Rockport by the Rockport Granite Company. The track was extended from Lanesville to Pigeon Cove. It took four years to blast a tunnel to allow the Great Arch to be built. This 65-foot span includes a keystone inscribed "September 29, 1872," indicating the date it was set. The arch took 11 weeks to complete. The locomotive shown here is the *Nella*, named after Colonel French's wife. (SBHS.)

Nine

DOLLIVER'S NECK
LIFESAVING STATION
"NORMAN'S WOE"

Dolliver's Neck Lifesaving Station was created in 1900 because of the many shipwrecks experienced in the area. Local residents remembered ships like *Mary D. Babson* and *D.P. Gale*, driven out of the harbor in the severe gale of March 21, 1861; the loss of the schooner *John P. Hale*, wrecked in the same place 12 years later, on November 17, 1873; and the schooner *Connaught Ranger*, wrecked on October 20, 1873. (CAM.)

The first keeper at Dolliver's Neck was Capt. Nelson F. King, who served there until Prohibition days. Walter Marchant was a substitute keeper and served as a surfman under Captain King in 1900. Pay was $60 a month, with each man providing his own food. There were two watches on patrol, one going east as far as Pavilion Beach and the other going to Rafe's Chasm. Here, the lifeboat is launched at Pavilion Beach in 1900. (CAM.)

Gloucester   Coast   Guard   Aug 6, 1939   1/50 F/6   3

By 1957, the lifeboat station had a complement of 13 men. The station's six boats included the following: a 40-foot utility boat, a 36-foot double-ender motor lifeboat, two self-bailing unsinkable motor surfboats, a 19-foot fisherman's dory, and a small skiff. (CAM.)

In February 1898, Fresh
Water Cove was the scene
of one of the worst marine
tragedies in the history
of Cape Ann. During the
famous "Portland Storm"
nor'easter, three ships were
wrecked against the rocks
at Dolliver's Neck, and a
yacht, the *Jumbo*, sank in
the cove. The destroyed
ships were the three-
masted schooner *George
W. Jewett* of Portland, on
which all hands were lost;
the schooner *Marcellus*
of Bucksport, Maine;
and the *James Holmes* of
Belfast, Maine. (CAM.)

Norman's Woe is a rock reef just off Dolliver's. It was the common dread of mariners seeking
Gloucester Harbor for protection. Gales were so fierce that ships would drag their anchors and
drift toward this reef. Such was the gale of 1839, which was recounted in a narrative poem
by Henry Wadsworth Longfellow, *The Wreck of the Hesperus*. This reef is awash at high tide,
although its elevation is 23 feet at low tide, thus contributing to a high number of wrecks. (Library
of Congress.)

Fitz Henry Lane did a number of oil paintings in the area of Dolliver's Neck on the western side of Gloucester Harbor. This piece from 1862, entitled *The Western Shore with Norman's Woe*, is exhibited at the Cape Ann Museum. Lane searched out unexplored places of pristine natural beauty, such as Norman's Woe, Dolliver's Neck, Brace's Cove, and Coffin's Beach. (CAM.)

Gloucester, Mass. - Life Saving Crew at Drill, Dollivers Neck.

This Hugh C. Leighton Co. postcard is postmarked 1907 and features the lifesaving crew on breeches buoy practice. Dolliver's Neck Station was closed in 1973 and moved to the current US Coast Guard station at Harbor Loop on the inner harbor. (CAM.)

This postcard shows the Dolliver's Neck Station on Freshwater Cove. (Robert Ambrogi collection.)

Surfmen dressed in their cork life vests prepare to launch lifeboat No. 6 into the surf. This boat belonged to the Dolliver's Neck Lifesaving Station No. 6 along the Cape Ann coast. When the station was recommissioned as a USCG station, it was renumbered Coast Guard Station No. 23. (CAM.)

This aerial photograph shows the Gloucester Coast Guard station at Dolliver's Neck before it was moved to Gloucester Harbor in 1974. A 44-foot motor lifeboat lies at the launch way in the upper left. The Dolliver's Neck Lifesaving Station became the Gloucester Coast Guard Station No. 23 in 1936. (USCG.)

The old station at Old House Cove (Dolliver's Neck) had its own boat ramp. Here, the crew slides down the launch way en route to a rescue. The No. 23 on the bow indicates that the boat belonged to Dolliver's Neck Coast Guard Station No. 23. (USCG.)

Oar-propelled surfboats were launched from this boathouse, which was soon to be demolished. A new boathouse was built on the supports to the left of the building. The castle-like structure in the background is the old Hammond Estate, built by John Hays Hammond Sr. as a summer mansion in 1929. When he died, he willed it to the Catholic Church, and it became a retirement home for priests. (USCG.)

On December 21, 1962, during a driving snowstorm, amid subzero temperatures and low visibility, the 87-foot dragger *Katie D* lost power and drifted. She grounded on Rocky Neck. The Coast Guard was called from Dolliver's Neck and rescued eight fishermen that day. (USCG.)

This 36-foot Coast Guard motor lifeboat went aground on Niles Beach just after its men rescued the crew of the *Katie D.* The crew was able to abandon the rescue boat unharmed. (USCG.)

The new Gloucester station opened in 1974 on Harbor Loop. It included dock space for the 95-foot cutter *Cape Cross.* The men of the *Cape Cross* saved the crew of the fishing vessel *Chester Poling* in 1977 when she went aground just south of the harbor. Today, the station has two 47-foot self-righting motor lifeboats and two 25-foot fast-response boats capable of speeds of 45 knots. (USCG.)

BIBLIOGRAPHY

Cann, Donald, and John Galluzzo. *The Coast Guard in Massachusetts.* Charleston, SC: Arcadia Publishing, 2011.

Claflin, James. *Lighthouses and Lifesaving along the Massachusetts Coast.* Charleston, SC: Arcadia Publishing, 1998.

———. *Price List of Standard Articles from General Depot: Government Printing Office, Washington, DC, 1901.* Worcester, MA: Kenrick A. Claflin & Son, 2011.

Copeland, Melvin T., and Elliot C. Rogers. *Saga of Cape Ann.* Freeport, ME: The Bond Wheelwright Co., 1960.

D'Entremont, Jeremy. *The Lighthouses of Massachusetts.* Beverly, MA: Commonwealth Editions, 2007.

Erkkila, Barbara. *Hammers on Stone.* Woolrich, ME: TBW Books, 1980.

Garland, Joseph E. *Down to the Sea.* Boston: David R. Godine, 1983.

———. *The Gloucester Guide, a Stroll through Place and Time.* Rockport, MA: Protean Press, 1990.

Gleason, Sarah C. *Kindly Lights.* Boston: Beacon Press, 1991.

Gould, R.T. *The Case for the Sea-Serpent.* New York: G.P. Putnam & Sons, 1934.

Greenbaum, Dan. *Ten Pound Island—A Closer Look.* Gloucester, MA: Resources for Cape Ann-Eleanor Pope, 1975.

Grimes, George. *Water Under the Keel, Memoirs of a Sea Going Life.* Rockland, ME: Milk Island Press, Maine Publishing, 2011.

Hill, Benjamin D., and Winfield S. Nevins. *The North Shore of Massachusetts Bay.* 4th ed. Salem, MA: Illustrated Guide, 1881.

Kenny, Herbert A. *Cape Ann: Cape America.* Gloucester, MA: The Curious Traveler Press, 1971.

Morris, John N. *Alone at Sea: Gloucester in the Age of the Dorymen 1623–1939.* Beverly, MA: Commonwealth Editions, 2010.

Robinson, F.J.G. *Tragabigzana or Cape Ann.* Boston: The Progressive Print, 1935.

ABOUT THE THACHER ISLAND ASSOCIATION

The Thacher Island Association is a nonprofit 501-c(3) organization dedicated to the restoration and maintenance of the Cape Ann Light Station on Thacher Island, a National Historic Landmark, and Straitsmouth Island Light Station, a National Register site. Both are located off the coast of Rockport, Massachusetts. Its charter is to raise funds for this effort. The author's proceeds from the sale of this book go to the association. Volunteers work on both islands during the summer months, maintaining the scenic walking trails and the buildings. They also work to preserve and restore the historic structures and the island's unique natural attributes and to make them accessible to the public. For more information, visit the Web site at www.thacherisland.org. Anyone interested in joining or donating to the association can send their check to Thacher Island Association, Box 73, Rockport, MA, 01966. Fees are $30 for individual, $60 for family, $125 for corporate, and $500 for lifetime membership.

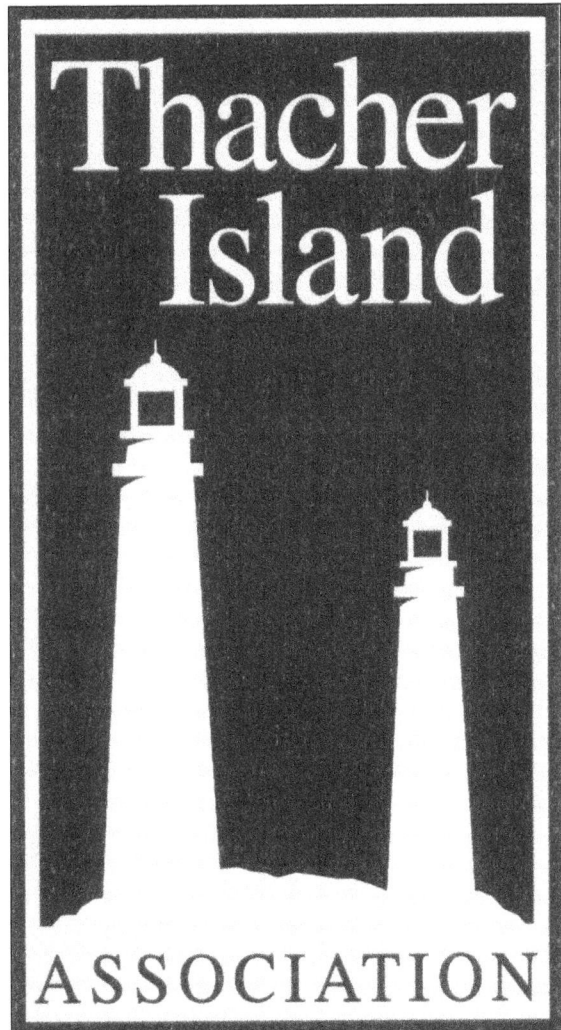

Visit us at
arcadiapublishing.com

www.ingramcontent.com/pod-product-compliance
Lightning Source LLC
Chambersburg PA
CBHW050647110426

42813CB00007B/1943